Latin Primer 3

Student Edition

LATIN PRIMER SERIES

Latin Primer: Book 1, Martha Wilson
Latin Primer 1: Student Edition
Latin Primer 1: Teacher's Edition
Latin Primer 1: Flashcard Set
Latin Primer 1: Audio Guide CD

Latin Primer: Book 2, Martha Wilson
Latin Primer 2: Student Edition
Latin Primer 2: Teacher's Edition
Latin Primer 2: Flashcard Set
Latin Primer 2: Audio Guide CD

Latin Primer: Book 3, Martha Wilson
Latin Primer 3: Student Edition
Latin Primer 3: Teacher's Edition
Latin Primer 3: Flashcard Set
Latin Primer 3: Audio Guide CD

Latin Primer: Book 4, Natali Monnette *(coming 2012)*
Latin Primer 4: Student Edition
Latin Primer 4: Teacher's Edition
Latin Primer 4: Flashcard Set
Latin Primer 4: Audio Guide CD

Latin Primer: Book 5, Natali Monnette *(coming 2013)*
Latin Primer 5: Student Edition
Latin Primer 5: Teacher's Edition
Latin Primer 5: Flashcard Set
Latin Primer 5: Audio Guide CD

Published by Canon Press
P.O. Box 8729, Moscow, ID 83843
800.488.2034 | www.canonpress.com

Martha Wilson, *Latin Primer Book 3 Student Edition*
First Edition 1994, Second Edition 1997, Third Edition 2011

Cover design by Rachel Hoffmann.
Interior layout and design by Phaedrus Media.
Typesetting by Laura Storm.
Printed in the United States of America.

11 12 13 14 15 16   10 9 8 7 6 5 4 3 2 1

Library of Congress Cataloging-in-Publication Data
Wilson, Martha.
  Latin primer. Book 3 / Martha Wilson ; edited by Laura Storm. -- 3rd ed., student ed.
      p. cm.
  ISBN-13: 978-1-59128-087-3 (pbk.)
  ISBN-10: 1-59128-087-7 (pbk.)
  1. Latin language--Grammar--Problems, exercises, etc I. Storm, Laura, 1981- II. Title.
  PA2087.5.W49324 2011
  478.2'421--dc22
                              2011013088

BOOK 3

Latin
PRIMER

MARTHA WILSON / Edited by LAURA STORM

canonpress
Moscow, Idaho

Contents

Unit 1: Weeks 1–8   2

Unit 2: Weeks 9–16   71

Unit 3: Weeks 17–24   145

Unit 4: Weeks 25–32   219

Appendices   293

INTRODUCTION

Discipulī,

If I were writing this to your parents or your teacher, I would point out the important Latin vocabulary and concepts and corresponding English vocabulary and grammar in this third primer. That would be honest, but I will appeal to you on different grounds: I think this will be fun for you.

My mother aims for a quality she calls "zip" in her potato salad, and she almost always achieves it. Laura Storm's work as editor has added that quality to this text by how she has supplemented the vocabulary and translation work. Her additions to the vocabulary are often entertaining. Her sentences are not boring. Perhaps my favorite is *Sine būtūrō sōlum sumus animālia* (!), but there is a general liveliness to them which I think you will appreciate.

One last comment before I leave you to this primer. My observation has been that the most diligent students enjoy their studies the most. Perhaps this is just the echo of my memory of the comment of C.S. Lewis that "the laziest boy in the class is the one who works hardest in the end . . . later, when they are preparing for an exam, that lazy boy is doing hours and hours of miserable drudgery over things the other boy [who took trouble] understands, and positively enjoys, in a few minutes."[1] Take the trouble to learn and memorize day by day, week by week. Not only will you do better in Latin, you will enjoy it more.

Valēte,
Martha Wilson

1. C.S. Lewis, *Mere Christianity* (New York: MacMillan, 1960), 168.

PRONUNCIATION GUIDE

Vowels

Vowels in Latin have only two pronunciations, long and short. When speaking, long vowels are held twice as long as short vowels. Long vowels are marked with a "macron" or line over the vowel (e.g., ā). Vowels without a macron are short vowels.

When spelling a word, including the macron is important, as it can determine the meaning of the word (e.g., *liber* is a noun meaning "book," and *līber* is an adjective meaning "free").

Long Vowels:

ā   like *a* in *father*: frāter, suprā
ē   like *e* in *obey*: trēs, rēgīna
ī   like *i* in *machine*: mīles, vīta
ō   like *o* in *holy*: sōl, glōria
ū   like *oo* in *rude*: flūmen, lūdus
ȳ   like *i* in *chip:* grȳps, cȳgnus

Short Vowels:

a   like *a* in *idea*: canis, mare
e   like *e* in *bet*: et, terra
i   like *i* in *this*: hic, silva
o   like *o* in *domain*: bonus, nomen
u   like *u* in *put*: sum, sub

Diphthongs

A combination of two vowel sounds collapsed together into one syllable is a dipthong:

ae   like *ai* in *aisle*   caelum, saepe
au   like *ou* in *house*   laudō, nauta
ei   like *ei* in *reign*   deinde
eu   like *eu* in *eulogy*   Deus
oe   like *oi* in *oil*   moenia, poena
ui   like *ew* in *chewy*   huius, hui

Consonants

Latin consonants are pronounced with the same sounds with the following exceptions:

c   like *c* in *come*   never soft like *city, cinema*, or *peace*
g   like *g* in *go*   never soft like *gem, geology*, or *gentle*
v   like *w* in *wow*   never like *Vikings, victor*, or *vacation*
s   like *s* in *sissy*   never like *easel, weasel*, or *peas*
ch   like *ch* in *chorus*   never like *church, chapel*, or *children*
r   is trilled   like a dog snarling, or a machine gun
i   like *y* in *yes*   when used before a vowel at the beginning of a word, between two vowels within a word; otherwise it's usually used as a vowel

1 UNIT ONE

UNIT 1: GOALS

Weeks 1–8

By the end of Unit 1, you should be able to . . .

- Chant from memory the first through fourth declension noun endings
- Recognize and distinguish first through fourth declension nouns
- Decline any first through fourth declension neuter noun
- Chant from memory the present, future, and imperfect verb ending chants
- Recognize and distinguish first, second, and third conjugation verbs
- Give the principal parts for any verb from the Word Lists
- Give a verb synopsis in the present, future, and imperfect tenses
- Compose and translate statements, questions, and commands using present, future, and imperfect active tenses (e.g., *Potestne mercātor lectum horrendum vendere?* means "Is the merchant able to sell the horrible couch?")
- Recognize predicate adjectives, predicate nouns, and direct objects, and know how to translate them into English or Latin

WEEK 1

Word List

NOUNS

1. audācia, -ae (f) . . . . boldness, courage
2. carrus, -ī (m) . . . . cart, wagon (two-wheeled)
3. cinis, cineris (m) . . . . ashes, destruction
4. collum, -ī (n) . . . . neck
5. culpa, -ae (f) . . . . fault, blame, sin
6. fenestra, -ae (f) . . . . window
7. nervus, -ī (m) . . . . tendon, nerve, sinew
8. ōs, ōris (n) . . . . mouth
9. rota, -ae (f) . . . . wheel
10. vultus, -ūs (m) . . . . face, expression

VERBS

11. amō, amāre, amāvī, amātum . . . . I love
12. currō, currere, cucurrī, cursum . . . . I run
13. dūcō, dūcere, dūxī, ductum . . . . I lead
14. properō, properāre, properāvī, properātum . . . I hurry, hasten, accelerate
15. sedeō, sedēre, sēdī, sessum . . . . I sit
16. videō, vidēre, vīdī, vīsum . . . . I see

ADVERBS

17. bene . . . . well
18. nōn . . . . not

Chants:

Present Active Verb Endings

LATIN			ENGLISH		
	SINGULAR	**PLURAL**		**SINGULAR**	**PLURAL**
1ST	-ō	-mus		I am *verbing*	we are *verbing*
2ND	-s	-tis		you are *verbing*	you all are *verbing*
3RD	-t	-nt		he/she/it is *verbing*	they are *verbing*

Future Active Verb Endings

LATIN			ENGLISH		
	SINGULAR	**PLURAL**		**SINGULAR**	**PLURAL**
1ST	-bō	-bimus		I will *verb*	we will *verb*
2ND	-bis	-bitis		you will *verb*	you all will *verb*
3RD	-bit	-bunt		he/she/it will *verb*	they will *verb*

Imperfect Active Verb Endings

LATIN			ENGLISH		
	SINGULAR	**PLURAL**		**SINGULAR**	**PLURAL**
1ST	-bam	-bāmus		I was *verbing*	we were *verbing*
2ND	-bās	-bātis		you were *verbing*	you all were *verbing*
3RD	-bat	-bant		he/she/it was *verbing*	they were *verbing*

Example of Third Conjugation Verb, *Dūcō*

PRESENT			FUTURE			IMPERFECT		
	SINGULAR	**PLURAL**		**SINGULAR**	**PLURAL**		**SINGULAR**	**PLURAL**
1ST	dūcō	dūcimus		dūcam	dūcēmus		dūcēbam	dūcēbāmus
2ND	dūcis	dūcitis		dūcēs	dūcētis		dūcēbās	dūcēbātis
3RD	dūcit	dūcunt		dūcet	dūcent		dūcēbat	dūcēbant

 Quotation:

meā culpā—"through my fault"

[This page intentionally blank]

Weekly Worksheet 1

name: _____

A. Fill in the blanks.

1. A verb shows _____ or _____.

2. How do you find a verb's stem? _____

3. To find out which conjugation a verb is in, you look at its _____.

4. First conjugation verb stems end in _____. All first conjugation verbs conjugate like

_____.

5. Second conjugation verb stems end in _____. All second conjugation verbs conjugate like

_____.

6. Third conjugation verb stems end in _____. All third conjugation verbs conjugate like

_____.

B. Answer the questions. Then conjugate *properō* in the present tense and translate it. Then conjugate it in the future and imperfect tenses.

1. Give the four principal parts of *properō:* _____

2. What is the stem of *properō?* _____

3. Which conjugation is it in? _____

Present

LATIN			ENGLISH		
	SINGULAR	PLURAL		SINGULAR	PLURAL
1ST					
2ND					
3RD					

Future

	SINGULAR	PLURAL
1ST		
2ND		
3RD		

Imperfect

	SINGULAR	PLURAL

C. Answer the questions. Then conjugate *sedeō* in the present, imperfect, and future tenses and translate it.

1. Give the four principal parts of *sedeō:* _____

2. What is the stem of *sedeō?* _____

3. Which conjugation is it in? _____

Present

LATIN   ENGLISH

	SINGULAR	PLURAL		SINGULAR	PLURAL
1ST					
2ND					
3RD					

Future

LATIN   ENGLISH

	SINGULAR	PLURAL		SINGULAR	PLURAL
1ST					
2ND					
3RD					

Imperfect

LATIN

	SINGULAR	PLURAL
1ST		
2ND		
3RD		

ENGLISH

	SINGULAR	PLURAL

D. Answer the questions. Then conjugate *dūcō* in the present, imperfect, and future tenses. Give the English translation for the imperfect tense.

1. Give the four principal parts of *dūcō:* _____

2. What is the stem of *dūcō?* _____

3. Which conjugation is it in? _____

Present

	SINGULAR	PLURAL
1ST		
2ND		
3RD		

Future

	SINGULAR	PLURAL

Imperfect

LATIN

	SINGULAR	PLURAL
1ST		
2ND		
3RD		

ENGLISH

	SINGULAR	PLURAL

E. Give the genitive singular form, gender (M, F, or N), and the English translation for each Latin noun.

	NOUN	GENITIVE SINGULAR	GENDER	TRANSLATION
1.	collum			
2.	cinis			
3.	vultus			
4.	audācia			
5.	carrus			
6.	ōs			
7.	rota			

F. Give an English derivative for each of these words. Remember, a derivative is an English word with a Latin root.

1. carrus _____

2. videō _____

3. nervus _____

4. collum _____

G. Latin's present tense can be translated into English in three different ways. For example, *olefactō* can be translated "I smell," "I do smell," or "I am smelling." Using *olefactō* as an example, write three translations for each verb.

1. videō _____

2. dūcō_____

3. amō _____

H. Fill in the blanks.

1. A singular verb takes a _____ subject noun.

2. A _____ verb takes a plural subject noun.

3. An _____ modifies a _____, adjective, or another adverb and answers

questions like *how?, where?, when?,* and *to what extent?*

I. Translate these sentences into English.

1. Culpa nōn amat. _____

2. Audācia dūcet. _____

3. Carrus nōn properābit! _____

4. Bene currēbātis. _____

5. Nōn bene videō. _____

J. Answer the question about this week's quotation.

1. What does *meā culpā* mean in English? _____

[This page intentionally blank]

WEEK 2

Word List

NOUNS

1. ānulus, -ī (m) . . . . ring
2. argentum, -ī (n). . . . . silver, money
3. campus, -ī (m). . . . . plain, athletic field, level area
4. capillus, -ī (m) . . . . hair
5. cervix, cervīcis (f). . . . . . . neck, nape (of neck)
6. cuspis, cuspidis (f) . . . . . . point (esp. of a spear)
7. digitus, -ī (m) . . . . finger, inch
8. fluvius, -ī (m) . . . . river
9. hērōs, hērōis (m) . . . . hero
10. index, indicis (m) . . . . informer, sign, forefinger
11. mola, -ae (f) . . . . millstone
12. palma, -ae (f) . . . . palm (of the hand), palm tree
13. patella, -ae (f) . . . . plate, dish
14. poena, -ae (f) . . . . penalty, punishment
15. pollex, pollicis (m) . . . . . thumb

VERBS

16. dēbeō, dēbēre, dēbuī, dēbitum. . . . . I owe, ought
17. lūceō, lūcēre, lūxī, — . . . . I shine, am bright
18. portō, portāre, portāvī, portātum . . . I carry
19. possum, posse, potuī, — . . . . I am able, can
20. rīdeō, rīdēre, rīsī, rīsum . . . . I laugh

Chant:

Present Active of *Possum* (Irregular Verb)

LATIN				ENGLISH		
	SINGULAR	PLURAL			SINGULAR	PLURAL
1ST	possum	possumus			I am able, can	we are able
2ND	potes	potestis			you are able	you all are able
3RD	potest	possunt			he/she/it is able	they are able

Quotation:

sub poenā—"under penalty"

Weekly Worksheet 2

name:

A. Fill in the blanks.

1. _____ express _____ or state of being.

2. In a Latin sentence, the verb is usually at the _____.

3. In a Latin question, the first word is usually the _____.

4. To form a question in Latin, _____ is added to the _____ word in the sentence.

B. Change each statement into a question, then translate the question into English.

	STATEMENT	QUESTION	TRANSLATION
1.	Lūcent.		
2.	Vidēs.		
3.	Potes.		
4.	Currēmus.		
5.	Rīdēbātis.		
6.	Dēbēbō.		
7.	Bene dūcēbat.		

C. Fill in the principal parts for each verb, then circle each verb's stem. At the end of the line, write whether the verb is in first (1), second (2), or third (3) conjugation.

1. dēbeō, _____, _____, _____ (_____)

2. currō, _____, _____, _____ (_____)

3. lūceō, _____, _____, _____ (_____)

4. portō, _____, _____, _____ (_____)

5. sedeō, _____, _____, _____ (_____)

6. videō, _____, _____, _____ (_____)

7. rīdeō, _____, _____, _____ (_____)

D. Fill in the blanks.

1. When you tell a dog, "Sit!", you're giving him a _____.

2. Is a command a noun, a verb, or an adjective? _____

3. Another word for "command" is _____.

4. To give a Latin command, you first need to find the verb's _____.

5. To give a singular command, what do you add to the stem? _____

6. To give a plural command using a first or second conjugation verb, what do you add to the

stem? _____

7. How do you give a plural command using a third conjugation verb? _____

_____

E. Turn each verb into a singular command and a plural command in Latin. Then translate the plural command into English.

	VERB	SINGULAR COMMAND	PLURAL COMMAND	TRANSLATION
1.	sedeō			
2.	amō			
3.	lūceō			
4.	currō			
5.	videō			
6.	portō			
7.	dūcō			
8.	properō			

F. Fill in the blanks.

1. The second principal part of a verb is also called the _____.

2. Does every regular verb have a second principal part? _____

G. Translate the following infinitives into English.

1. vidēre _____   3. lūcēre _____

2. portāre _____   4. posse _____

H. Translate these infinitives into Latin.

1. to owe _____   4. to lead _____

2. to run _____   5. to love _____

3. to sit _____   6. to laugh _____

I. Each of these short sentences uses an infinitive. First, find the main verb, then underline the infinitive, and translate the sentence.

1. Ānulus lūcēre dēbet. _____

2. Amāre potestis. _____

3. Potesne properāre? _____

4. Potestne ōs rīdēre? _____

5. Currere dēbēmus! _____

6. Index bene nōn potest vidēre. _____

J. For each noun, give the genitive singular form, gender (M, F, or N), and translation.

	NOUN	GENITIVE	GENDER	TRANSLATION
1.	mola			
2.	ānulus			

	NOUN	GENITIVE	GENDER	TRANSLATION
3.	argentum			
4.	fluvius			
5.	patella			
6.	cervix			
7.	digitus			
8.	campus			
9.	pollex			
10.	collum			

K. Each of the words below comes from a Latin root! Figure out which of your Latin words is the root, and then give its English meaning.

	ITALIAN	SPANISH	FRENCH	LATIN	ENGLISH
1.	colpa	culpa	culpabilité		
2.	anello	anillo	anneau		
3.	eroe	héroe	héros		

L. Answer the questions about this week's quotation.

1. What does *sub poenā* mean? _____

2. In English, these two Latin words have become _____ word.

2. A subpoena is a _____ .

WEEK 3

Word List

NOUNS

1. āla, -ae (f) . . . . wing
2. astrum, -ī (n). . . . . star, constellation
3. aurum, -ī (n) . . . . gold
4. avāritia, -ae (f). . . . . greed
5. fūmus, -ī (m). . . . . smoke
6. humus, -ī (f) . . . . ground, soil
7. incola, -ae (m/f). . . . . inhabitant, settler, colonist
8. laurus, -ī (f) . . . . laurel tree
9. oppidum, -ī (n) . . . . town
10. pecūnia, -ae (f) . . . . money
11. praemium, -ī (n) . . . . prize, reward
12. prōvincia, -ae (f). . . . . . . province
13. ventus, -ī (m). . . . . wind
14. vīta, -ae (f) . . . . life

ADJECTIVES

15. densus, -a, -um . . . . dense, thick
16. horrendus, -a, -um . . . . . . horrible, dreadful, awful
17. trepidus, -a, -um . . . . trembling, anxious, frightened
18. ūmidus, -a, -um . . . . wet, damp, moist

VERBS

19. mereō, merēre, meruī, meritum. . . . . I deserve, earn, am worthy of
20. regnō, regnāre, regnāvī, regnātum. . . I rule, govern, reign

Chants:

First Declension Noun Endings

	LATIN			ENGLISH	
	SINGULAR	PLURAL		SINGULAR	PLURAL
NOMINATIVE	-a	-ae		a, the *noun*	the *nouns*
GENITIVE	-ae	-ārum		of the *noun*, the *noun's*	of the *nouns*, the *nouns'*
DATIVE	-ae	-īs		to, for the *noun*	to, for the *nouns*
ACCUSATIVE	-am	-ās		the *noun*	the *nouns*
ABLATIVE	-ā	-īs		by, with, from the *noun*	by, with, from the *nouns*

Second Declension Noun Endings

	LATIN			ENGLISH	
	SINGULAR	PLURAL		SINGULAR	PLURAL
NOM.	-us	-ī		a, the *noun*	the *nouns*
GEN.	-ī	-ōrum		of the *noun*, the *noun's*	of the *nouns*, the *nouns'*
DAT.	-ō	-īs		to, for the *noun*	to, for the *nouns*
ACC.	-um	-ōs		the *noun*	the *nouns*
ABL.	-ō	-īs		by, with, from the *noun*	by, with, from the *nouns*

Second Declension Neuter Noun Endings

	LATIN			ENGLISH	
	SINGULAR	PLURAL		SINGULAR	PLURAL
NOM.	-um	-a		a, the *noun*	the *nouns*
GEN.	-ī	-ōrum		of the *noun*, the *noun's*	of the *nouns*, the *nouns'*
DAT.	-ō	-īs		to, for the *noun*	to, for the *nouns*
ACC.	-um	-a		the *noun*	the *nouns*
ABL.	-ō	-īs		by, with, from the *noun*	by, with, from the *nouns*

Quotation:

ad astra per ālās porcī—"To the stars on the wings of a pig"

Weekly Worksheet 3

name: _____

A. Answer the questions. Then label and complete the chants.

1. What is the definition of a noun? _____

2. How do you find the base of a noun? _____

_____

3. What case does a Latin subject noun take? _____

_____ DECLENSION

	SINGULAR	PLURAL
NOM.		
GEN.	-ae	
DAT.		
ACC.		
ABL.		

_____ DECLENSION

	SINGULAR	PLURAL
NOM.		
GEN.	-ī	
DAT.		
ACC.		
ABL.		

_____ DECLENSION _____

	SINGULAR	PLURAL
NOM.		-a
GEN.		
DAT.		
ACC.		
ABL.		

4. You can tell what declension a noun is in by looking at its _____ .

5. Which declension is *humus, -ī* in? _____

6. Which declension is *prōvincia, -ae* in? _____

7. Which declension is *aurum, -ī* in? _____

B. Label each noun's declension (1 or 2) and gender (M, F, or N). Then decline it.

DECLENSION _____ GENDER _____

	SINGULAR	PLURAL
NOM.	ventus	
GEN.		
DAT.		
ACC.		
ABL.		

DECLENSION _____ GENDER _____

	SINGULAR	PLURAL
NOM.	āla	
GEN.		
DAT.		
ACC.		
ABL.		

DECLENSION _____ GENDER _____

	SINGULAR	PLURAL
NOM.	astrum	
GEN.		
DAT.		
ACC.		
ABL.		

DECLENSION _____ GENDER _____

	SINGULAR	PLURAL
NOM.	laurus	
GEN.		
DAT.		
ACC.		
ABL.		

C. For each noun, give its genitive singular form, gender (M, F, or N), base, and translation.

	NOUN	GENITIVE	GENDER	BASE	TRANSLATION
1.	aurum				
2.	humus				
3.	praemium				
4.	vīta				
5.	pecūnia				

D. Fill in the blanks.

1. An adjective _____ a _____ or pronoun.

2. An adjective answers the questions _____ kind? _____ one? or how

   _____?

3. It matches the subject noun in _____, _____, and _____.

4. In Latin sentences, does the adjective usually come before or after the noun? _____

5. Adjectives that decline like first and second declension nouns are called _____

   _____.

6. Adjectives can be paired with nouns from _____ declension.

E. Decline *densus, -a, -um* in the neuter and *trepidus, -a, -um* in the feminine.

	SINGULAR	PLURAL
NOM.		
GEN.		
DAT.		
ACC.		
ABL.		

	SINGULAR	PLURAL
NOM.		
GEN.		
DAT.		
ACC.		
ABL.		

F. Decline the phrase *the wet laurel tree.*

	SINGULAR	PLURAL
NOM.		
GEN.		
DAT.		
ACC.		
ABL.		

G. Underline the adjective that goes with the subject noun and then translate the phrase.

NOUN	ADJECTIVE	TRANSLATION
1. Ventus	horrendus / horrendum	_____
2. Ālae	ūmidīs / ūmidae	_____
3. Incola	trepidam / trepida	_____
4. Capillī	horrendus / horrendī	_____
5. Astra	densa / densae	_____
6. Humus	ūmidus / ūmida	_____
7. Fūmus	densus / densa	_____
8. Oppidum	trepidus / trepidum	_____

H. Each of the following words comes from a Latin root! Figure out which of your Latin words is the root, and then give its English meaning.

	ITALIAN	SPANISH	FRENCH	LATIN	ENGLISH
1.	ala	ala	aile		
2.	fumo	humo	fumée		
3.	premio	premio	prix		

I. Answer the following questions about derivatives from this week's Word List. The derivatives are italicized.

1. The English word *humble* comes from the Latin word _____.

2. If someone has been *humbled,* he has literally been brought low to the _____.

3. The English word *avarice* comes from the Latin word _____.

4. *Avarice* is _____, a selfish, wrongful desire for money and riches.

J. Translate these sentences into English.

1. Incola ūmidus ridēbat._____

2. Mereōne dūcere? _____

3. Astra densa lūcēbunt. _____

4. Prōvincia horrenda regnāre nōn potest. _____

WEEK 4

Word List

NOUNS

1. arcus, -ūs (m) . . . . bow, arch, rainbow

2. bōs, bovis (m/f) . . . . ox, bull, cow

3. cornū, -ūs (n) . . . . horn

4. exercitus, -ūs (m) . . . . army

5. gelū, -ūs (n) . . . . chill, frost

6. genū, -ūs (n) . . . . knee

7. gladiātor, gladiātōris (m) . . . gladiator

8. gradus, -ūs (m) . . . . step, pace

9. latus, lateris (n) . . . . flank, side

10. leō, leōnis (m) . . . . lion

11. regiō, regiōnis (f) . . . . . . region, direction, area

12. sanguis, sanguinis (m) . . . . blood

13. tīgris, tīgridis (m/f) . . . . . tiger

14. verū, -ūs (n) . . . . javelin, spit (for roasting meat)

15. vulnus, vulneris (n) . . . . . . wound

ADJECTIVES

16. ferus, -a, -um . . . . fierce, wild

17. longus, -a, -um . . . . long

VERBS

18. pugnō, pugnāre, pugnāvī, pugnātum . . . I fight

19. rudō, rudere, rudīvī, rudītum . . . . I roar, bellow, bray

CONJUNCTIONS

20. et . . . . and

Chants:

Third Declension Noun Endings

	LATIN			ENGLISH	
	SINGULAR	**PLURAL**		**SINGULAR**	**PLURAL**
NOM.	**x**	-ēs		a, the *noun*	the *nouns*
GEN.	-is	-um		of the *noun*, the *noun's*	of the *nouns*, the *nouns'*
DAT.	-ī	-ibus		to, for the *noun*	to, for the *nouns*
ACC.	-em	-ēs		the *noun*	the *nouns*
ABL.	-e	-ibus		by, with, from the *noun*	by, with, from the *nouns*

Third Declension Neuter Noun Endings

	LATIN			ENGLISH	
	SINGULAR	**PLURAL**		**SINGULAR**	**PLURAL**
NOM.	**x**	-a		a, the *noun*	the *nouns*
GEN.	-is	-um		of the *noun*, the *noun's*	of the *nouns*, the *nouns'*
DAT.	-ī	-ibus		to, for the *noun*	to, for the *nouns*
ACC.	**x**	-a		the *noun*	the *nouns*
ABL.	-e	-ibus		by, with, from the *noun*	by, with, from the *nouns*

Fourth Declension Noun Endings

	LATIN			ENGLISH	
	SINGULAR	**PLURAL**		**SINGULAR**	**PLURAL**
NOM.	-us	-ūs		a, the *noun*	the *nouns*
GEN.	-ūs	-uum		of the *noun*, the *noun's*	of the *nouns*, the *nouns'*
DAT.	-uī	-ibus		to, for the *noun*	to, for the *nouns*
ACC.	-um	-ūs		the *noun*	the *nouns*
ABL.	-ū	-ibus		by, with, from the *noun*	by, with, from the *nouns*

Fourth Declension Neuter Noun Endings

	LATIN			ENGLISH	
	SINGULAR	PLURAL		SINGULAR	PLURAL
NOM.	-ū	-ua		a, the *noun*	the *nouns*
GEN.	-ūs	-uum		of the *noun*, the *noun's*	of the *nouns*, the *nouns'*
DAT.	-ū	-ibus		to, for the *noun*	to, for the *nouns*
ACC.	-ū	-ua		the *noun*	the *nouns*
ABL.	-ū	-ibus		by, with, from the *noun*	by, with, from the *nouns*

Quotation:

Christiānōs ad leōnem!—"The Christians to the lion!"

[This page intentionally blank]

Weekly Worksheet 4

name:

A. Answer the questions.

1. What is the definition of a noun? _____

2. How do you find the base of a noun? _____

_____

B. Label each noun's declension (1, 2, 3, or 4) and gender (M, F, or N). Then decline it.

DECLENSION _____ GENDER _____

	SINGULAR	PLURAL
NOM.	regiō	
GEN.		
DAT.		
ACC.		
ABL.		

DECLENSION _____ GENDER _____

	SINGULAR	PLURAL
NOM.	latus	

DECLENSION _____ GENDER _____

	SINGULAR	PLURAL
NOM.	exercitus	
GEN.		
DAT.		
ACC.		
ABL.		

DECLENSION _____ GENDER _____

	SINGULAR	PLURAL
NOM.	genū	

C. Underline the adjective that goes with the subject noun and then translate the phrase.

NOUN	ADJECTIVE	TRANSLATION
1. Cornua	longum / longa	_____
2. Leōnēs	ūmidī / ūmidae	_____
3. Regiō	densa / densus	_____
4. Gelū	horrendus / horrendum	_____
5. Gladiātor	ferus / ferī	_____
6. Exercitūs	trepidus / trepidī	_____
7. Ventus	ferum / ferus	_____
8. Latus	ūmidum / ūmidus	_____

D. Decline the phrase *the wild bull*. (Remember, *bōs* declines irregularly in the plural!)

	SINGULAR	PLURAL
NOM.		
GEN.		
DAT.		
ACC.		
ABL.		

E. Conjugate *rudō* in the future and imperfect tenses.

Future

	SINGULAR	PLURAL
1ST		
2ND		
3RD		

Imperfect

	SINGULAR	PLURAL
1ST		
2ND		
3RD		

F. For each noun, list its genitive singular, gender, declension, and English translation.

	NOUN	GENITIVE	GENDER	DECLENSION	ENGLISH
1.	sanguis				
2.	verū				
3.	arcus				
4.	vulnus				
5.	laurus				

G. Underline the noun that goes with the verb and then translate the sentences.

NOUN	VERB	TRANSLATION
1. Bovis / Bovēs	rudunt.	_____
2. Gladiātor / Gladiātorēs	pugnābit.	_____
3. Sanguis / Sanguinēs	currēbat.	_____
4. Exercitus / Exercitūs	properābant.	_____
5. Tīgris / Tīgridēs	sedent.	_____

H. Answer the questions about this week's quotation.

1. What does *Christiānōs ad leōnem!* mean? _____

2. Why was this a popular saying in Roman regions? _____

_____

3. What is the case and number of *leōnem?* _____

I. Translate these Latin sentences into English.

1. Hērōs ferus regnāre potest. _____

2. Meretne pugnāre gladiātor trepidus? _____

_____

3. Leōnēs ferī et tīgridēs horrendī rudunt et pugnānt. _____

_____

4. Aurum, argentum, ānulī, et praemia lūcēbant. _____

_____

5. Pollex et digitī portāre possunt. _____

6. Gradus nōn properābit. _____

7. Sedēte et rīdēte! _____

8. Exercitus ūmidus nōn bene pugnābat. _____

_____

J. Draw a line to match each derivative with its Latin root. (If you need help, look up the meaning of the derivative in a dictionary!)

1. sanguine   ferus

2. unicorn   gradus

3. arch   genū

4. gradual   ūmidus

5. feral   densus

6. humid   arcus

7. condensate   cornū

8. genuflect   sanguis

WEEK 5

Word List

NOUNS

1. coma, -ae (f) . . . . hair, leaves, fleece, mane

2. coturnix, coturnīcis (f) . . . . . quail

3. equus, -ī (m) . . . . horse

4. flōs, flōris (m) . . . . flower

5. fulmen, fulminis (n) . . . . . . thunderbolt, lightning

6. harēna, -ae (f) . . . . sand

7. lapis, lapidis (m) . . . . stone, rock

8. lūcus, -ī (m) . . . . grove

9. pinna, -ae (f) . . . . feather

10. silva, -ae (f) . . . . forest

11. tempestās, tempestātis (f) . . weather, storm

ADJECTIVES

12. clārus, -a, -um . . . . clear, loud, bright

13. quiētus, -a, -um . . . . quiet, sleeping, peaceful

VERBS

14. agitō, agitāre, agitāvī, agitātum . . . . I drive, arouse, disturb

15. ardeō, ardēre, arsī, arsum . . . . I blaze, burn

16. candeō, candēre, canduī, — . . . . I glow, am white

17. dēlectō, dēlectāre, dēlectāvī, dēlectātum . . . I delight

18. sonō, sonāre, sonuī, sonitum . . . . I resound, sound, make a noise

19. sum, esse, fuī, futūrum . . . . I am

20. terreō, terrēre, terruī, territum . . . . I frighten, terrify

Chants:

Present Active of *Sum* (Irregular Verb)

LATIN

ENGLISH

	SINGULAR	PLURAL		SINGULAR	PLURAL
1ST	sum	sumus		I am	we are
2ND	es	estis		you are	you all are
3RD	est	sunt		he/she/it is	they are

Future Active of *Sum*

LATIN

ENGLISH

	SINGULAR	PLURAL		SINGULAR	PLURAL
1ST	erō	erimus		I will be	we will be
2ND	eris	eritis		you will be	you all will be
3RD	erit	erunt		he/she/it will be	they will be

Imperfect Active of *Sum*

LATIN

ENGLISH

	SINGULAR	PLURAL		SINGULAR	PLURAL
1ST	eram	erāmus		I was	we were
2ND	erās	erātis		you were	you all were
3RD	erat	erant		he/she/it was	they were

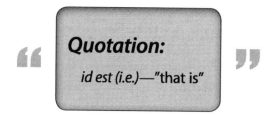

" **Quotation:** **"**

id est (i.e.)—"that is"

Weekly Worksheet 5   *name:*

A. Fill in the principal parts for each verb.

1. sonō, _____, _____, _____

2. possum, _____, _____, _____

3. _____, _____, terruī, _____

4. mereō, _____, _____, _____

5. _____, candēre, _____, _____

6. dēlectō, _____, _____, dēlectātum

7. _____, _____, _____, regnātum

8. ardeō, _____, _____, _____

9. _____, _____, rudīvī, _____

10. _____, agitāre, _____, _____

B. Answer the following questions about *sum*. Then conjugate and translate *sum* in the present, future, and imperfect tenses.

1. Which conjugation is *sum* in? _____

_____

2. What are the four principal parts of *sum*? _____

Present Active

	LATIN			ENGLISH	
	SINGULAR	PLURAL		SINGULAR	PLURAL
1ST					
2ND					
3RD					

Future Active

LATIN

ENGLISH

	SINGULAR	PLURAL		SINGULAR	PLURAL
1ST					
2ND					
3RD					

Imperfect Active

LATIN

ENGLISH

	SINGULAR	PLURAL		SINGULAR	PLURAL
1ST					
2ND					
3RD					

C. Give the Latin for each of these English phrases.

1. under penalty _____

2. that is _____

3. through my fault _____

4. The Christians to the lion! _____

5. To the stars on the wings of a pig_____

D. Use the vocabulary from this week's Word List to complete the definition of these English derivatives.

1. An *incandescent* light bulb _____.

    a) is large   b) glows with heat   c) is expensive

2. A *sylvan* place _____.

    a) has woods   b) has fairies   c) has mountains

3. A *lapidary* inscription is _____.

    a) lengthy   b) engraved on stone   c) incorrect

4. *Floriculture* is the cultivation of _____.

    a) manners   b) vegetables   c) flowers

E. Fill in the blanks.

1. An _____ modifies a noun or pronoun.

2. An adjective answers the questions _____ kind? _____ one? or how

_____?

3. In Latin, a _____ adjective follows a linking verb and describes a subject noun.

4. It matches the subject noun in _____, _____, and _____.

5. Give an example in Latin of a linking verb: _____

6. A predicate noun follows a linking verb and identifies or renames the _____ noun.

7. Which Latin case do you use for the predicate noun? _____

8. Which Latin case do you use for the subject? _____

9. In Latin sentences with predicate adjectives and nouns, does the verb usually appear at the

beginning, in the middle, or at the end of the sentence? _____

F. Translate these sentences into English.

1. Praemium est pecunia. _____

2. Fulmen clārum candet. _____

3. Regiō longa est provincia. _____

4. Erantne coturnīcēs quiētae? _____

5. Lūcī erant ūmidī et densī. _____

6. Potesne agitāre? _____

7. Equī ferī sunt trepidī et currunt. _____

8. Incola ferus dēbet esse hērōs. _____

9. Poena est horrenda. _____

10. Tempestās nōn est quiēta. _____

G. Translate these sentences into Latin. (Hint: Watch for gender, number, and case!)

1. The region is a dense forest. _____

2. The smoke will be thick and horrible. _____

3. Were the stones bright? _____

H. Underline the ending of each verb. Then translate it, and give its person (1, 2, or 3), number (S or P), and tense (present, future, imperfect).

	VERB	TRANSLATION	PERSON	NUMBER	TENSE
1.	sumus				
2.	rudit				
3.	candēbam				
4.	eritis				
5.	dēlectābātis				
6.	merēbis				

I. Decline the phrase *a bright stone.*

	SINGULAR	PLURAL
NOM.		
GEN.		
DAT.		
ACC.		
ABL.		

[This page intentionally blank]

WEEK 6

Word List

NOUNS

1. aedificium, -ī (n) . . . . building
2. caterva, -ae (f) . . . . crowd, mob
3. dominus, -ī (m) . . . . master, lord
4. epulae, -ārum (f, pl.) . . . . . feast
5. famula, -ae (f) . . . . maid, servant (female)
6. famulus, -ī (m) . . . . servant (male)
7. frūmentum, -ī (n) . . . . grain, (pl.) crops
8. hortus, -ī (m) . . . . garden
9. locus, -ī (m) . . . . place
10. via, -ae (f) . . . . road, street, way

ADJECTIVES

11. citus, -a, -um . . . . fast, quick
12. fessus, -a, -um . . . . tired, weary
13. perītus, -a, -um . . . . skilled, experienced
14. raucus, -a, -um . . . . hoarse

VERBS

15. dēmonstrō, dēmonstrāre, dēmonstrāvī, dēmonstrātum. . . I show, point out
16. emō, emere, ēmī, emptum. . . . . I buy, purchase
17. habeō, habēre, habuī, habitum . . . . I have, hold
18. parō, parāre, parāvī, parātum . . . . I prepare
19. torreō, torrēre, torruī, tostum . . . . I burn, parch, dry up
20. vītō, vītāre, vītāvī, vītātum . . . . I avoid

Chant:

No new chant this week.

Quotation:

Via trīta, via tūta—"The well-worn way, the safe way"

Weekly Worksheet 6

name:

A. Fill in the blanks.

1. The word that *receives the action of the verb* is called the _____.

2. Which Latin case do you use for this part of speech? _____

3. Which Latin case do you use for the subject? _____

B. Label each noun's declension (1, 2, or 3) and gender (M, F, or N). Then decline it.

DECLENSION _____ GENDER _____

	SINGULAR	PLURAL
NOM.	aedificium	
GEN.		
DAT.		
ACC.		
ABL.		

DECLENSION _____ GENDER _____

	SINGULAR	PLURAL
NOM.	via	
GEN.		
DAT.		
ACC.		
ABL.		

DECLENSION _____ GENDER _____

	SINGULAR	PLURAL
NOM.	flōs	
GEN.		
DAT.		
ACC.		
ABL.		

DECLENSION _____ GENDER _____

	SINGULAR	PLURAL
NOM.	arcus	
GEN.		
DAT.		
ACC.		
ABL.		

Now, go back through the nouns you've just declined and circle the accusative endings of each one.

B. For each noun, list its genitive singular form, gender, declension, and its singular and plural accusative forms.

	NOUN	GENITIVE	GENDER	DECL.	SINGULAR ACCUSATIVE	PLURAL ACCUSATIVE
1.	harēna					
2.	coturnix					
3.	lūcus					
4.	fulmen					
5.	lapis					
6.	gradus					
7.	bōs					
8.	cornū					
9.	aurum					
10.	avāritia					
11.	laurus					
12.	vulnus					
13.	pinna					
14.	equus					
15.	ōs					

C. Give the accusative of each word.

1. flowers _____

2. feast _____

3. thunderbolt _____

4. faces _____

5. crowd _____

6. chills _____

7. places _____

8. grain _____

D. These sentences have direct objects, which will be in the accusative case. For each sentence, underline the subject noun(s) and circle the direct object(s), then translate the sentence.

1. Caterva aedificium torrēre parat! _____

_____

2. Incola fessa harēnam vidēbit. _____

3. Famulī frūmentum emere nōn possunt. _____

_____

4. Exercitum tempestās terret. _____

5. Equus citus lapidēs portābit. _____

6. Ventus raucus hortum agitābat. _____

_____

7. Habetne equus ālās et pinnās? _____

8. Tīgridēs gladiātor pugnābat et terrēbat. _____

_____

9. Incola quietum locum dēmonstrat. _____

10. Avāritia dominum horrendum regnat. _____

E. Translate these English sentences into Latin.

1. I was frightening the crowds. _____

2. Fight the lions! (sg.) _____

3. A thunderbolt ought to burn the place. _____

4. Will the garden have flowers? _____

F. On the lines below, give the Latin word for each picture!

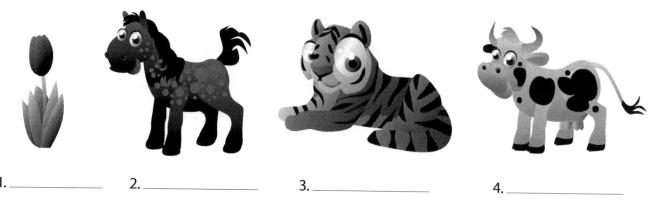

1. _____ 2. _____ 3. _____ 4. _____

G. Answer the following questions about this week's quotation.

1. What does *via trīta, via tūta* mean? _____

2. What is the case and number of *via?* _____

H. Answer these questions about derivatives. You may use a dictionary, an encyclopedia, and/or the internet.

1. *Torrid* is a derivative of the Latin word _____.

2. The Torrid Zone is the region of the earth's surface between the tropics of Cancer and Capricorn.

Why is it called the Torrid Zone?_____

_____

3. *Raucous* is a derivative of the Latin word _____.

4. Look up *raucous* and give its definition:_____

Macaronic Verse: Carmen Possum

A *macaronic* poem or story jumbles together two or more languages (often one of them is Latin). You will probably need your Latin dictionary on hand to translate this humorous poem.

Carmen Possum

Author Unknown

The nox was lit by lux of Luna,
And 'twas a nox most opportuna
To catch a possum or a coona;
For nix was scattered o'er this mundus,
A shallow nix, et non profundus.
On sic a nox with canis unus,
Two boys went out to hunt for coonus.
The corpus of this bonus canis
Was full as long as octo span is,
But brevior legs had canis never
Quam had hic dog; et bonus clever.
Some used to say, in stultum jocum
Quod a field was too small locum
For sic a dog to make a turnus
Circum self from stem to sternus.
Unus canis, duo puer,
Nunquam braver, nunquam truer,
Quam hoc trio numquam fuit,
If there was I never knew it.
This bonus dog had one bad habit,
Amabat much to tree a rabbit,
Amabat plus to chase a rattus,
Amabat bene tree a cattus.
But on this nixy moonlight night
This old canis did just right.
Numquam treed a starving rattus,

Numquam chased a starving cattus,

But sucurrit on, intentus

On the track and on the scentus,

Till he trees a possum strongum,

In a hollow trunkum longum.

Loud he barked in horrid bellum,

Seemed on terra vehit pellum.

Quickly ran the duo puer

Mors of possum to secure.

Quam venerit, one began

To chop away like quisque man.

Soon the axe went through the truncum

Soon he hit it all kerchunkum;

Combat deepens, on ye braves!

Canis, pueri et staves

As his powers non longius carry,

Possum potest non pugnare.

On the nix his corpus lieth.

Down to Hades spirit flieth,

Joyful pueri, canis bonus,

Think him dead as any stonus.

Now they seek their pater's domo,

Feeling proud as any homo,

Knowing, certe, they will blossom

Into heroes, when with possum

They arrive, narrabunt story,

Plenus blood et plenior glory.

Pompey, David, Samson, Caesar,

Cyrus, Black Hawk, Shalmanezer!

Tell me where est now the gloria,

Where the honors of victoria?

Nunc a domum narrent story,

Plenus sanguine, tragic, gory.

Pater praiseth, likewise mater,

Wonders greatly younger frater.

Possum leave they on the mundus,

Go themselves to sleep profundus,

Somniunt possums slain in battle,

Strong as ursae, large as cattle.

When nox gives way to lux of morning,

Albam terram much adorning,

Up they jump to see the varmin',

Of the which this is the carmen.

Lo! possum est resurrectum!

Ecce pueri dejectum,

Ne relinquit back behind him,

Et the pueri never find him.

Cruel possum! bestia vilest,

How the pueros thou beguilest!

Pueri think non plus of Caesar,

Go ad Orcum, Shalmanezer,

Take your laurels, cum the honor,

Since ista possum is a goner!

Macaronic Verse: Composition

These lines are for you to write a macaronic story or poem with English and Latin words, using vocabulary you've learned in this book, as well as other Latin words you already know. Try to put Latin subjects, direct objects, and predicate nouns in their correct case.

WEEK 7

Word List

NOUNS

1. coniunx, coniugis (m/f) . . . . spouse, wife, husband
2. custōs, custōdis (m/f) . . . . . guard, watchman
3. flamma, -ae (f) . . . . flame
4. lectus, -ī (m) . . . . couch, bed
5. lūcerna, -ae (f) . . . . lamp
6. mensa, -ae (f) . . . . table
7. mercātor, mercātōris (m) . . . merchant, trader
8. sella, -ae (f) . . . . seat, chair

ADJECTIVES

9. acūtus, -a, -um . . . . sharp, pointed, intelligent
10. bonus, -a, -um . . . . good
11. fīdus, -a, -um . . . . faithful, trustworthy
12. laetus, -a, -um . . . . happy, joyful, glad
13. malus, -a, -um . . . . bad, evil, wicked
14. novus, -a, -um . . . . new
15. publicus, -a, -um . . . . . . public
16. sumptuōsus, -a, -um . . . . . expensive

VERBS

17. convocō, convocāre, convocāvī, convocātum . . I call together
18. explōrō, explōrāre, explōrāvī, explōrātum . . . . I search out, explore
19. pergō, pergere, perrexī, perrectum . . . . I continue, proceed
20. vendō, vendere, vendidī, venditum . . . . I sell, advertise

Chant:

No new chant this week.

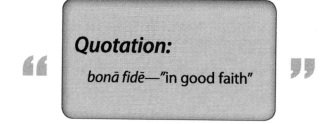

Quotation:

bonā fidē—"in good faith"

Weekly Worksheet 7

name: _____

A. Translate each word into Latin or English as appropriate.

1. custōs _____

2. seat _____

3. sumptuōsus _____

4. audācia _____

5. lamp _____

6. mercātor _____

7. wing _____

8. laetus _____

9. mensa _____

10. silver _____

11. latus _____

12. lectus _____

13. frūmenta _____

14. coma _____

15. bad _____

16. acūtus _____

B. Give a synopsis for each of the following verbs. A verb synopsis has two steps. First, write out all four principal parts for the verb. Second, give the verb forms specified and their translations.

1. *convocō* in the first person singular: _____

	LATIN	ENGLISH
PRESENT ACT.		
FUTURE ACT.		
IMPERFECT ACT.		

2. *vendō* in the second person plural: _____

	LATIN	ENGLISH
PRESENT ACT.		
FUTURE ACT.		
IMPERFECT ACT.		

3. *habeō* in the third person singular:_____

	LATIN	ENGLISH
PRESENT ACT.		
FUTURE ACT.		
IMPERFECT ACT.		

4. *explōrō* in the first person plural: _____

	LATIN	ENGLISH
PRESENT ACT.		
FUTURE ACT.		
IMPERFECT ACT.		

5. *pergō* in the second person singular: _____

	LATIN	ENGLISH
PRESENT ACT.		
FUTURE ACT.		
IMPERFECT ACT.		

C. Decline the phrase *the new lamp* in Latin.

	SINGULAR	PLURAL
NOM.		
GEN.		
DAT.		
ACC.		
ABL.		

D. Translate each phrase into its *nominative* form in Latin. (Hint: An adjective must match the noun it modifies in gender, number, and case, but *not* necessarily in declension.)

1. faithful watchman (m) _____

2. happy wife _____

3. happy husband _____

4. intelligent merchant _____

5. new couch _____

6. new buildings _____

7. peaceful gardens _____

8. long way _____

E. Translate each phrase into its *accusative* form in Latin.

1. public buildings _____

2. long roads _____

3. evil merchants _____

4. expensive table _____

5. public place _____

6. bright flames _____

7. happy wife _____

8. sharp watchmen (m) _____

F. Translate these sentences into English.

1. Mercātor lūcernās sumptuōsās et lectōs novōs vendit. _____

_____

57

2. Custōs malus mercātōrēs terrēre perget. _____

_____

3. Equus et bovēs epulās habēbant. _____

4. Famulus perītus frūmentum parābit. _____

_____

5. Coniunx mala et acūta tīgridēs ferōs agitābat. _____

_____

6. Fulmen citum custōdem quietum terret. _____

_____

7. Famulae fīdae epulās parābant. _____

_____

8. Novus carrus coniugem fessam portat. _____

9. Mercātor comam horrendam habēre pergit. _____

_____

10. Explōrā aedificium! _____

G. Translate these sentences into Latin.

1. Fierce flames burn up the garden. _____

2. The weary guards (m) were avoiding the mob. _____

_____

3. The couch is long and horrible. _____

4. A hoarse lion continues to roar. _____

H. Circle the correct answer by considering the Latin roots of these derivatives.

1. Circle the two correct definitions of *acute.*

a) not blunt   b) pretty   c) distant   d) shrewd   e) hilarious   f) rude

2. If something is *flammable* it _____.

a) is difficult to see   b) is pleasant to cook and eat   c) tends to ignite easily and burn rapidly

3. *Custody* is _____.

a) the act or right of guarding   b) the top of a chimney   c) a dessert

[This page intentionally blank]

WEEK 8

Word List

NOUNS

1. grex, gregis (m) . . . . flock, herd

2. vīsus, -ūs (m) . . . . view, sight

ADJECTIVES

3. cūriōsus, -a, -um . . . . curious, diligent

4. gelidus, -a, -um . . . . cold, icy, frosty

5. mīrus, -a, -um . . . . strange, wonderful

VERBS

6. tardō, tardāre, tardāvī, tardātum . . . . I delay, slow down

Chant:

No new chant this week.

Quotation:

No new quotation this week.

[This page intentionally blank]

Weekly Worksheet 8

name:

A. Translate each word into Latin or English as appropriate.

1. vīsus _____

2. densus _____

3. lapis _____

4. flame _____

5. capillus_____

6. joyful _____

7. skilled_____

8. sanguis _____

9. grex _____

10. collum _____

11. patella _____

12. nervus _____

13. pecūnia _____

14. pergō_____

15. strange_____

16. ring _____

17. loud _____

18. regiō _____

19. sella _____

20. mouth _____

21. gradus _____

22. wild _____

23. wife _____

24. mola_____

25. bene _____

26. curious_____

27. caterva_____

28. thumb _____

29. gelidus_____

30. anxious _____

B. Give a synopsis for each of the following verbs.

1. *sedeō* in the third person singular: _____

	LATIN	ENGLISH
PRESENT ACT.		
FUTURE ACT.		
IMPERFECT ACT.		

2. *tardō* in the second person plural: _____

	LATIN	ENGLISH
PRESENT ACT.		
FUTURE ACT.		
IMPERFECT ACT.		

3. *rudō* in the first person plural:_____

	LATIN	ENGLISH
PRESENT ACT.		
FUTURE ACT.		
IMPERFECT ACT.		

C. Conjugate and translate each verb in the given tense.

1. *ardeō* in the imperfect active

LATIN | ENGLISH

	SINGULAR	PLURAL	SINGULAR	PLURAL
1ST				
2ND				
3RD				

2. *emō* in the future active

LATIN | ENGLISH

	SINGULAR	PLURAL	SINGULAR	PLURAL
1ST				
2ND				
3RD				

D. Fill in the blanks.

1. A verb shows _____ or _____ .

2. How do you find a verb's stem? _____

3. To find out which conjugation a verb is in, you look at its _____ .

4. First conjugation verb stems end in _____ . All first conjugation verbs conjugate like

_____ .

5. Second conjugation verb stems end in _____ . All second conjugation verbs conjugate like

_____ .

6. Third conjugation verb stems end in _____ . All third conjugation verbs conjugate like

_____ .

7. To form a question in Latin, _____ is added to the _____ word in the sentence.

8. To give a plural command using a first or second conjugation verb, what do you add to the

stem? _____

9. How do you give a plural command using a third conjugation verb? _____

_____

10. What is the definition of a noun? _____

11. How do you find the base of a noun? _____

12. Which Latin case do you use for the subject? _____

13. An _____ modifies a noun or pronoun.

14. An adjective answers the questions _____ kind? _____ one? or how

_____ ?

15. In Latin, a _____ adjective follows a _____ verb and describes a

subject noun.

16. It matches the subject noun in _____, _____, and _____.

17. A _____ noun follows a linking verb and identifies or _____ the

subject noun.

18. Which Latin case do you use for a predicate noun? _____

19. The word that *receives the action of the verb* is called the _____.

20. Which Latin case do you use for this type of word? _____

E. Label each noun's declension (1, 2, 3, or 4) and gender (M, F, or N). Then decline it.

DECLENSION _____ GENDER _____

	SINGULAR	PLURAL
NOM.	vīsus	
GEN.		
DAT.		
ACC.		
ABL.		

DECLENSION _____ GENDER _____

	SINGULAR	PLURAL
NOM.	grex	
GEN.		
DAT.		
ACC.		
ABL.		

DECLENSION _____ GENDER _____

	SINGULAR	PLURAL
NOM.	ōs	
GEN.		
DAT.		
ACC.		
ABL.		

DECLENSION _____ GENDER _____

	SINGULAR	PLURAL
NOM.	verū	
GEN.		
DAT.		
ACC.		
ABL.		

DECLENSION _____ GENDER _____   DECLENSION _____ GENDER _____

	SINGULAR	PLURAL
NOM.	campus	
GEN.		
DAT.		
ACC.		
ABL.		

	SINGULAR	PLURAL
NOM.	culpa	
GEN.		
DAT.		
ACC.		
ABL.		

F. Decline the phrase *a quick pace* in Latin.

	SINGULAR	PLURAL
NOM.		
GEN.		
DAT.		
ACC.		
ABL.		

G. Use the vocabulary from the weekly Word Lists to complete the definition of these English derivatives.

1. An *aureate* evening is _____.

    a) golden   b) dark   c) windy

2. Something that is *ridiculous* might make you _____.

    a) sing   b) ride a horse   c) laugh

3. The *patella* is a _____-shaped bone covering the front of the knee.

    a) wing   b) dish   c) heart

4. A *cornucopia* is often called the _____ of plenty.

   a) stone   b) road   c) horn

H. Translate these sentences into English.

1. Lapidēs famulam tardābunt. _____

2. Grex cūriōsus aedificium mīrum explōrāre pergit. _____

_____

3. Equum ventus et fulminēs terrēbant. _____

_____

4. Mercātor perītus comās sumptuōsās vendēbat. _____

_____

5. Epulae erant longae et mīrae. _____

6. Potesne ventum habēre? _____

7. Coniunx bonus Dominum amat. _____

8. Index sanguinem gelidum et audāciam horrendam habet. _____

_____

9. Dēmonstrāte viam! _____

10. Tīgris cita verū longum pugnābit. _____

_____

11. Quietī erimus, nōn clārī. _____

12. Avāritia horrenda gladiātōrem agitat. _____

Translate these sentences into Latin.

13. The settlers will explore the new region. _____

14. Will you point out the new couches? _____

15. Flames will parch the thick grain. _____

16. The intelligent flock avoids the crowd. _____

17. Have a seat! (sg.) _____

I. Complete the Latin quotations, then give their meanings.

1. Christiānōs ad _____! : _____

2. mea _____ : _____

3. ad _____ per _____ porcī: _____

    _____

4. _____ fīde: _____

[This page intentionally blank]

2 UNIT TWO

UNIT 2: GOALS

Weeks 9–16

By the end of Unit 2, you should be able to . . .

- Recognize, decline, and translate third declension i-stem nouns
- Recognize, decline, and translate fifth declension nouns
- Recognize, decline, and translate personal pronouns (*ego, tū, nōs, vōs*)
- Give the principal parts for any verb from the Word Lists

WEEK 9

Word List

NOUNS

1. antrum, -ī (n) . . . . cave
2. collis, collis (m) . . . . hill
3. dens, dentis (m) . . . . tooth, tusk, fang
4. dracō, dracōnis (m) . . . . dragon
5. hostis, hostis (m/f) . . . . enemy, foe (of one's country)
6. monocerōs, monocerōtis (m) . . unicorn
7. nox, noctis (f) . . . . night
8. serpēns, serpentis (m/f) . . . . . snake, serpent
9. squāma, -ae (f) . . . . scale (of an animal)
10. unguis, unguis (m) . . . . fingernail, toenail, claw, hoof

ADJECTIVES

11. callidus, -a, -um . . . . clever, sly, cunning
12. celsus, -a, -um . . . . lofty, high
13. magicus, -a, -um . . . . magical
14. obscūrus, -a, -um . . . . hidden, dark

VERBS

15. calcitrō (1) . . . . I kick
16. mordeō, mordēre, momordī, morsum. . . I bite
17. mūtō (1) . . . . I change
18. oppugnō (1) . . . . I attack
19. spectō (1) . . . . I watch, look at

CONJUNCTIONS

20. sed. . . . . but

Chants:

Third Declension i-Stem Noun Endings: Masculine & Feminine

LATIN ENGLISH

	SINGULAR	PLURAL	SINGULAR	PLURAL
NOM.	x	-ēs	a, the *noun*	the *nouns*
GEN.	-is	**-ium**	of the *noun*, the *noun's*	of the *nouns,* the *nouns'*
DAT.	-ī	-ibus	to, for the *noun*	to, for the *nouns*
ACC.	-em	-ēs	the *noun*	the *nouns*
ABL.	-e	-ibus	by, with, from the *noun*	by, with, from the *nouns*

Examples of Masculine & Feminine Third Declension i-Stem Nouns

	SINGULAR	PLURAL		SINGULAR	PLURAL
NOM.	collis (x)	collēs		serpēns (x)	serpentēs
GEN.	collis	coll**ium**		serpentis	serpent**ium**
DAT.	collī	collibus		serpentī	serpentibus
ACC.	collem	collēs		serpentem	serpentēs
ABL.	colle	collibus		serpente	serpentibus

> ## Quotation:
>
> *Hīc sunt dracōnēs*—"Here are dragons"

Weekly Worksheet 9

name:

A. Complete the chant for this week and answer the questions about it.

	SINGULAR	PLURAL

1. This chant is for masculine and _____ third declension _____ nouns.

2. Which ending tells you a noun's declension? _____

3. The genitive ending for the third declension is _____.

4. Which ending in this chant is different from the regular third declension chant? _____

B. There are two questions you must ask to determine if a third declension noun is a *masculine or feminine* i-stem.

Question 1: Does the noun's nominative singular end in *-is* or *-ēs* **and** have the same number of syllables in the nominative and genitive singular? If so, then it's an i-stem.

Question 2: Does the noun's nominative singular end in *-s* or *-x* **and** have a base ending in two consonants? If so, then it's an i-stem.

Below are masculine and feminine third declension nouns. Using the questions above, tell whether each noun is an i-stem (Yes or No) and if it is, which question tells you so (1 or 2).

1. vestis, vestis _____

2. mors, mortis _____

3. ratis, ratis _____

4. mōns, mōntis _____

5. pater, patris _____

6. avis, avis _____

7. fōns, fontis _____

8. adulēscēns, adulēscēntis _____

9. lītus, lītoris _____

10. nāvis, nāvis _____

C. Answer the questions, then decline *collis* and *dens* in the charts below.

1. Which declension are *collis* and *dens* in? _____

2. Are they regular or i-stem nouns? _____

	SINGULAR	PLURAL
NOM.	collis	
GEN.		
DAT.		
ACC.		
ABL.		

	SINGULAR	PLURAL
NOM.	dens	
GEN.		
DAT.		
ACC.		
ABL.		

D. Label each noun's declension (1, 2, 3, 3i, or 4) and gender (M, F, or N). Then decline it.

DECLENSION _____ GENDER _____

	SINGULAR	PLURAL
NOM.	dracō	
GEN.		
DAT.		
ACC.		
ABL.		

DECLENSION _____ GENDER _____

	SINGULAR	PLURAL
NOM.	unguis	
GEN.		
DAT.		
ACC.		
ABL.		

DECLENSION _____ GENDER _____

	SINGULAR	PLURAL
NOM.	fulmen	
GEN.		
DAT.		
ACC.		
ABL.		

DECLENSION _____ GENDER _____

	SINGULAR	PLURAL
NOM.	nox	
GEN.		
DAT.		
ACC.		
ABL.		

E. Decline the phrase *the clever serpent* (masc.) in Latin.

	SINGULAR	PLURAL
NOM.		
GEN.		
DAT.		
ACC.		
ABL.		

F. Give the masculine, feminine, and neuter nominative singular of these adjectives in Latin.

	ADJECTIVE	MASCULINE	FEMININE	NEUTER
1.	magical			
2.	dark			
3.	cold			
4.	lofty			

G. Give a synopsis for each of the following verbs.

1. *calcitrō* in the second person plural: _____

	LATIN	ENGLISH
PRESENT ACT.		
FUTURE ACT.		
IMPERFECT ACT.		

2. *mordeō* in the third person singular: _____

	LATIN	ENGLISH
PRESENT ACT.		
FUTURE ACT.		
IMPERFECT ACT.		

H. Fill in the principal parts for each verb.

1. oppugnō, _____, _____, _____

2. mūtō, _____, _____, _____

3. spectō, _____, _____, _____

I. Translate these sentences into English.

1. Monocerōs magicus collēs celsōs explōrābat. _____

_____

2. Monocerōs antra obscūra bene vītābat._____

_____

3. Sed dracō citus spectat et oppugnat!_____

_____

4. Dracō dentēs acūtōs dēmonstrat et ālās horrendās. _____

_____

5. Monocerōs callidus nōn est trepidus._____

6. Dracōnem malum calcitrābit et mordēbit._____

_____

7. Dracō vulnera habet et pugnāre nōn potest. _____

_____

8. Erit gelidus et quiētus. _____

9. Monocerōs et collēs sunt laetī. _____

10. Potesne dracōnēs pugnāre? _____

Translate these sentences into Latin.

11. Are horses able to have horns? _____

12. The night was long and dark, and I was tired. _____

_____

13. Snakes have scales and long fangs. _____

_____

14. The hidden ring was changing the foe. _____

15. Change the wheels! (pl.) _____

J. Answer the questions about this week's quotation.

1. What does the phrase *Hīc sunt dracōnēs* mean? _____

2. Where does this phrase originally appear? _____

_____

3. Near what continent does it appear? _____

K. Give a derivative for each of the following words.

1. dens _____

2. mūtō _____

[This page intentionally blank]

WEEK 10

Word List

NOUNS

1. animal, animālis (n) . . . . . . animal
2. avis, avis (f) . . . . bird
3. canis, canis (m/f) . . . . dog
4. fēlēs, fēlis (f) . . . . cat
5. fōns, fontis (m) . . . . spring, fountain, source
6. iter, itineris (n) . . . . journey, road, route, trek
7. mare, maris (n) . . . . sea
8. mōns, mōntis (m) . . . . . . mountain
9. ratis, ratis (f) . . . . raft
10. rēte, rētis (n) . . . . net

ADJECTIVES

11. cārus, -a, -um . . . . dear, beloved, favorite
12. longinquus, -a, -um . . . . . far away, distant
13. magnus, -a, -um . . . . large, big, great
14. parvus, -a, -um . . . . little, small, unimportant

VERBS

15. caveō, cavēre, cāvī, cautum . . . . I am wary of, take care, am on guard against
16. errō (1) . . . . I wander, err, am mistaken
17. nāvigō (1) . . . . I sail
18. vehō, vehere, vexī, vectum . . . . I carry, convey

ADVERBS

19. paene . . . . almost
20. sōlum . . . . only

Chants:

Third Declension i-Stem Noun Endings: Neuter

LATIN   ENGLISH

	SINGULAR	PLURAL		SINGULAR	PLURAL
NOM.	x	**-ia**		a, the *noun*	the *nouns*
GEN.	-is	**-ium**		of the *noun*, the *noun's*	of the *nouns*, the *nouns'*
DAT.	-ī	-ibus		to, for the *noun*	to, for the *nouns*
ACC.	x	**-ia**		the *noun*	the *nouns*
ABL.	**-ī**	-ibus		by, with, from the *noun*	by, with, from the *nouns*

Examples of Neuter Third Declension i-Stem Nouns

	SINGULAR	PLURAL		SINGULAR	PLURAL
NOM.	animal (x)	animal**ia**		mare (x)	mar**ia**
GEN.	animalis	animal**ium**		maris	mar**ium**
DAT.	animalī	animalibus		marī	maribus
ACC.	animal (x)	animal**ia**		mare (x)	mar**ia**
ABL.	animalī	animalibus		marī	maribus

Quotation:

Cavē canem—"Beware of the dog"

Weekly Worksheet 10   *name:*

A. Complete the chant for third declension neuter i-stems, and answer the questions about it.

	SINGULAR	PLURAL
NOM.		
GEN.		
DAT.		
ACC.		
ABL.		

1. Which ending tells you a noun's declension? _____

2. The genitive ending for the third declension is _____.

3. How many endings in this chant are different from the regular third declension chant? _____

B. Last week you learned two i-stem questions. This week, the third and final question tells you whether a noun is a *neuter* i-stem. (Remember: Ask this question only after you know the noun is in the third declension *and* is neuter.)

Question 3: Does the neuter noun's nominative singular end in *-al, -ar,* or *-e?* If so, then it's a neuter i-stem.

Below are neuter third declension nouns. Using the question above, tell whether each noun is a neuter i-stem (Yes or No).

1. toral, torālis _____   5. rēte, rētis _____

2. calcar, calcāris _____   6. tribūnal, tribūnālis _____

3. iter, itineris _____   7. exemplar, exempāris _____

4. nāvāle, nāvālis _____   8. corpus, corporis _____

Below are third declension nouns. Using all three i-stem questions, tell whether each noun is an i-stem (Yes or No), and if it is, which question tells you (1, 2, or 3). You will need to use your dictionary.

1. dracō, dracōnis _____   2. cornix, cornicis _____

3. nox, noctis _____

7. unguis, unguis _____

4. rāmāle, rāmālis _____

8. dens, dentis _____

5. īgnis, īgnis _____

9. cōnsul, cōnsulis _____

6. sedīle, sedīlis _____

10. cubital, cubitālis _____

C. Answer the questions, then decline *rēte* and *animal* in the chart below.

1. Which declension are *rēte* and *animal* in? _____

2. Are they regular or i-stem nouns? _____

3. What is their gender? _____

	SINGULAR	PLURAL
NOM.	rēte	
GEN.		
DAT.		
ACC.		
ABL.		

	SINGULAR	PLURAL
NOM.	animal	
GEN.		
DAT.		
ACC.		
ABL.		

D. Label each noun's declension (1, 2, 3, 3i, or 4) and gender (M, F, or N). Then decline it. Do as much as you can from memory!

DECLENSION _____ GENDER _____

	SINGULAR	PLURAL
NOM.	avis	
GEN.		
DAT.		
ACC.		
ABL.		

DECLENSION _____ GENDER _____

	SINGULAR	PLURAL
NOM.	canis	
GEN.		
DAT.		
ACC.		
ABL.		

DECLENSION _____ GENDER _____   DECLENSION _____ GENDER _____

	SINGULAR	PLURAL
NOM.	latus	
GEN.		
DAT.		
ACC.		
ABL.		

	SINGULAR	PLURAL
NOM.	fōns	

E. Decline the phrase *the little sea* in Latin.

	SINGULAR	PLURAL
NOM.		
GEN.		
DAT.		
ACC.		
ABL.		

F. Give a synopsis for each of the following verbs.

1. *nāvigō* in the first person singular: _____

	LATIN	ENGLISH
PRESENT ACT.		
FUTURE ACT.		
IMPERFECT ACT.		

2. *vehō* in the second person plural:_____

	LATIN	ENGLISH
PRESENT ACT.		
FUTURE ACT.		
IMPERFECT ACT.		

3. *errō* in the third person singular:_____

	LATIN	ENGLISH
PRESENT ACT.		
FUTURE ACT.		
IMPERFECT ACT.		

G. Underline the adjective that goes with the noun (watch the cases!), and then translate the phrase.

NOUN	ADJECTIVE	TRANSLATION
1. Animal	cārus / cārum	_____
2. Mōntēs	parvōs / parva	_____
3. Mare	ferum / fera	_____
4. Rētia	magna / magnam	_____
5. Avis	sumptuōsus / sumptuōsa	_____
6. Fontēs	magicās / magicī	_____
7. Ratis	cita / citus	_____
8. Unguēs	mīrī / mīrae	_____

H. Answer the questions about this week's quotation.

1. What does *Cavē canem* mean? _____

2. Is this a statement or a command? _____

3. Is the verb directed at one person or multiple people? _____

4. What would be the plural form of the verb? _____

5. What declension is *canem?* _____

6. What is its number and case? _____

I. Translate these sentences into English.

1. Canis et fēlēs maria nāvigābant. _____

2. Animālia ratem parvam et rēte habent. _____

_____

3. Canis magnus fēlem nōn terret. _____

4. Sed fēlēs parva canem cavēbit. _____

_____

3. Ratis errat, et maria fera ratem vehunt. _____

_____

4. Canis spectat et harenam dēmonstrat. _____

_____

5. Fēlēs callida avēs parvās et fontem longinquum videt, sed canis mōntem sōlum videt. _____

_____

_____

6. Canis parat explōrāre, sed fēlēs parat oppugnāre canem cūriōsum. _____

_____

7. Fēlēs canem paene mordet, sed canis dentēs vītābit. _____

_____

8. Canis nōn est laetus, sed fēlēs mala rīdet. _____

_____

9. Fēlēs rudit, "Cavē fēlem!" _____

Translate these sentences into Latin.

10. The settler will only explore the high mountain. _____

_____

11. The journey was long and horrible. _____

12. The bird is on guard against the bad, beloved cat. _____

_____

13. The lion almost sees the hidden flock. _____

14. The new horses have large hooves and long manes. _____

_____

15. The Lord rules the stars, the seas, and the mountains. _____

_____

K. Each of the words below comes from a Latin root! Figure out which of your Latin words is the root, and then give its English meaning.

	ITALIAN	SPANISH	FRENCH	LATIN	ENGLISH
1.	animale	animal	animal		
2.	montagna	montaña	montagne		
3.	mare	mar	mer		

[This page intentionally blank]

Crossword

Complete the crossword puzzle! Write in the Latin word for each clue. (None of the Latin words in the puzzle or in the clues have macrons.)

ACROSS

Put each word in the number and case given. Translate italicized words into Latin.

1. rota in nominative plural

4. *greed* in nominative singular

7. provincia in accusative singular

9. *smoke* in accusative singular

11. *cat* in dative plural

12. incola in accusative singular

13. *I love*

14. *constellation* in nominative plural

15. serpens in nominative plural

16. campus in nominative plural

17. *window* in accusative plural

18. *wind* in accusative plural

19. laurus in accusative plural

20. *I purchase*

21. *tooth* in nominative singular

28. *money* in nominative singular

29. *region* in accusative singular

31. oppidum in nominative plural

32. poena in accusative plural

35. *reward* in accusative plural

36. *ground, soil* in nominative singular

37. *toenail* in genitive plural

38. dracō in accusative plural

39. *only*

DOWN

Translate the italicized word into Latin. You'll need to watch its function in the sentence to get the case right!

1. They watched the *rafts* from the bluff.

2. They could see the *spring* between the rocks.

3. Her *hair* is long.

5. The captain noticed the *boldness* of the boy.

6. The *storm* came suddenly.

8. *Groves* of aspen trees grew on the hillsides.

9. Jack picked the *flower*.

10. They remembered few *storms* as harsh as this.

13. The *silver* was very shiny.

15. *Forests* covered all the islands.

16. The *clear* view was beautiful.

17. *Thunderbolts* lit the entire valley.

22. The *horse* kicked up its heels.

23. The *heroes* returned from the war.

24. The jeweler admired the *stone*.

25. A bandit stopped the *wagons*.

26. The *sin* was great.

27. The explorers saw the *sands* of Egypt.

30. Cloudy *mountains* stood beyond the fields.

33. The *night* was long and quiet.

34. Two deer crossed the *river* at dusk.

35. Five years in jail was the *punishment*.

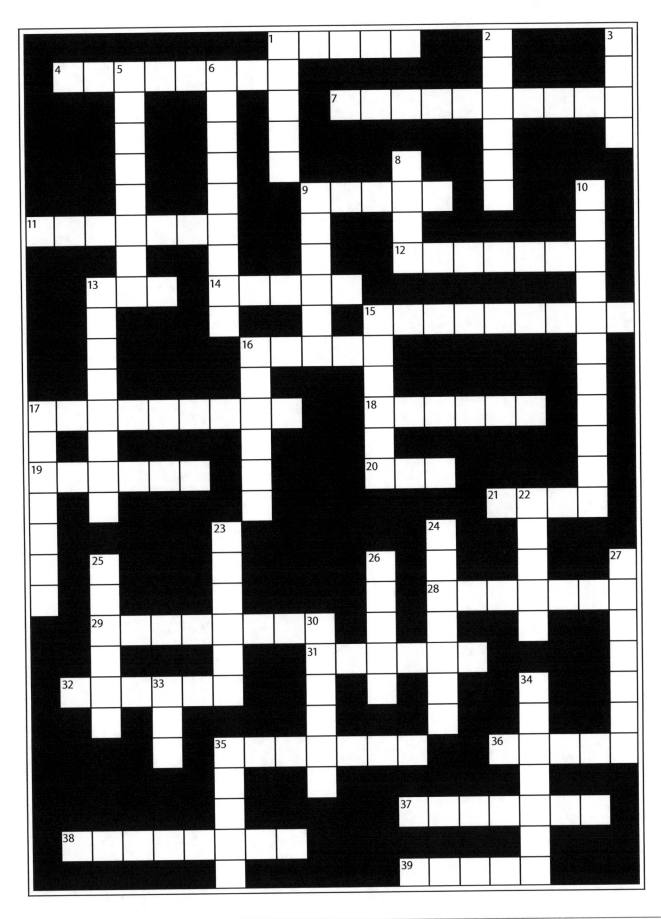

[This page intentionally blank]

WEEK 11

Word List

NOUNS

1. cāseus, -ī (m) . . . . cheese
2. cēna, -ae (f) . . . . dinner, meal
3. cibus, -ī (m) . . . . food
4. dōnum, -ī (n) . . . . gift
5. lac, lactis (n) . . . . milk
6. lactūca, -ae (f) . . . . lettuce
7. lardum, -ī (n) . . . . bacon, lard
8. macula, -ae (f) . . . . spot, mark, stain
9. pānis, pānis (m) . . . . bread
10. vīnum, -ī (n) . . . . wine

ADJECTIVES

11. albus, -a, -um . . . . white, pale
12. brūnus, -a, -um . . . . brown
13. caeruleus, -a, -um . . . . . blue
14. flāvus, -a, -um . . . . yellow, blond
15. niger, nigra, nigrum . . . . black, dark
16. ruber, rubra, rubrum . . . . red

VERBS

17. dō, dare, dedī, datum . . . . I give
18. gustō (1) . . . . I taste
19. laudō (1) . . . . I praise
20. rogō (1) . . . . I ask

Chant:

No new chant this week.

Quotation:

Deōrum cibus est—"It is food for gods"

Weekly Worksheet 11

name:

A. Complete the chants for third declension masculine/feminine and neuter i-stems.

MASCULINE/FEMININE

	SINGULAR	PLURAL
NOM.		
GEN.		
DAT.		
ACC.		
ABL.		

NEUTER

	SINGULAR	PLURAL

Now in each chant, go through and circle the endings that are different from the standard third declension and third declension neuter chants.

B. You've learned three questions to identify whether a third declension noun is an i-stem. Fill in the blanks to complete the questions.

1. Does the noun's nominative singular end in _____ or _____ *and* have the

_____ number of _____ in the nominative and _____ singular?

If so, then it _____ an i-stem.

2. Does the noun's nominative singular end in _____ or _____ *and* have a base ending in

_____ _____? If so, then it is an _____.

3. Does the _____ noun's nominative singular end in _____, _____, or

_____? If so, then it is a _____ i-stem.

C. Using the i-stem questions, tell whether each of the following nouns is an i-stem (Yes or No), and if it is, which question tells you so (1, 2, or 3).

1. pānis, pānis _____

2. lac, lactis _____

3. dens, dentis _____

4. rēte, rētis _____

5. collis, collis _____

6. grex, gregis _____

7. canis, canis _____

8. nox, noctis _____

9. cēna, -ae _____

10. animal, animālis _____

11. hostis, hostis _____

12. mōns, mōntis _____

13. serpēns, serpentis _____

14. unguis, unguis _____

15. mare, maris _____

16. fēlēs, fēlis _____

D. Label each noun's declension (1, 2, 3, 3i, or 4) and gender (M, F, or N). Then decline it. Do as much as you can from memory!

DECLENSION _____ GENDER _____

	SINGULAR	PLURAL
NOM.	cāseus	
GEN.		
DAT.		
ACC.		
ABL.		

DECLENSION _____ GENDER _____

	SINGULAR	PLURAL
NOM.	avis	

DECLENSION _____ GENDER _____

	SINGULAR	PLURAL
NOM.	lac	
GEN.		
DAT.		
ACC.		
ABL.		

DECLENSION _____ GENDER _____

	SINGULAR	PLURAL
NOM.	rēte	
GEN.		
DAT.		
ACC.		
ABL.		

DECLENSION _____ GENDER _____

	SINGULAR	PLURAL
NOM.	macula	
GEN.		
DAT.		
ACC.		
ABL.		

DECLENSION _____ GENDER _____

	SINGULAR	PLURAL
NOM.	bōs	
GEN.		
DAT.		
ACC.		
ABL.		

E. Decline the phrase *white bread* in Latin.

	SINGULAR	PLURAL
NOM.		
GEN.		
DAT.		
ACC.		
ABL.		

F. Give a synopsis for each of the following verbs.

1. *gustō* in the second person singular: _____

	LATIN	ENGLISH
PRESENT ACT.		
FUTURE ACT.		
IMPERFECT ACT.		

2. *rogō* in the third person plural: _____

	LATIN	ENGLISH
PRESENT ACT.		
FUTURE ACT.		
IMPERFECT ACT.		

3. *dō* in the first person plural: _____

	LATIN	ENGLISH
PRESENT ACT.		
FUTURE ACT.		
IMPERFECT ACT.		

G. Underline the adjective that goes with the noun (watch the endings—the nouns could be nominative or accusative, singular or plural!), and then translate the phrase.

NOUN	ADJECTIVE	TRANSLATION
1. cāseum	acūtum / acūtus	_____
2. maculae	parvam / parvae	_____
3. fēlēs	brūnus / brūna	_____

NOUN	ADJECTIVE	TRANSLATION
4. lac	album / alba	_____
5. cēna	cārus / cāra	_____
6. vīnum	ruber / rubrum	_____
7. lardum	mīram / mīrum	_____
8. noctēs	nigrae / nigrōs	_____
9. lactūcae	magnae / magnās	_____
10. canēs	flava / flavōs	_____

H. Answer the questions about this week's quotation.

1. What does *Deōrum cibus est* mean? _____

2. What is the person, number, and tense of *est?*_____

4. What is the number and case of *deōrum?* _____

5. What is the number and case of *cibus?*_____

6. What is *cibus's* function in the sentence? _____

I. Each sentence is missing a Latin word. Complete the sentences by translating the words in parentheses into Latin. Then translate the entire sentence into English.

1. Aurum delectat (the dragons) _____._____

_____

2. (Taste, sg.) _____ flāvōs et albōs cāseōs! _____

_____

3. (The river) _____ tardābit incolās._____

_____

4. Custōdēs laudābant (the bacon) _____. _____

_____

5. Tempestās nōn terret (the unicorn) _____. _____

_____

6. (The black bird) _____ _____ est clāra et rauca. _____

_____

7. (I will give) _____ sōlum parvum dōnum. _____

_____

8. Gregēs (love) _____ flōrēs et lactūcās. _____

_____

J. Translate these sentences into English.

1. Serpentēsne parvī sunt caeruleī? _____

2. Coniunx bona lardum, pānem, et cāseum emet. _____

_____

3. Pānem album amō, sed pānem brūnum nōn gustābō. _____

_____

4. Flammae horrendae lactūcam torrēbant, sed nōn lapidēs. _____

_____

5. Mare longinquum et nigrum dōnum malum vehit. _____

_____

Translate these sentences into Latin.

6. I do not see blue cheese, but I will buy white wine._____

_____

7. The bread is thick, and the bacon is almost magical. _____

_____

8. The cats are only tasting the cold milk. _____

_____

K. On the lines below, give the Latin word for each picture!

1._____   2._____   3._____   4._____

5._____   6._____   7._____   8._____

[This page intentionally blank]

WEEK 12

Word List

NOUNS

1. cunīculus, -ī (m) . . . . rabbit
2. diēs, diēī (m) . . . . day, period of time
3. effigiēs, effigiēī (f) . . . . image, likeness, statue
4. fidēs, fideī (f) . . . . faith, trust
5. hōrologium, hōrologiī (n) . . . clock, watch
6. merīdiēs, merīdiēī (m) . . . . . noon, midday
7. puella, -ae (f) . . . . girl
8. rēgīna, -ae (f) . . . . queen
9. rēs, reī (f) . . . . thing
10. rēx, rēgis (m) . . . . king
11. spēs, speī (f) . . . . hope
12. tempus, temporis (n) . . . . . time

ADJECTIVES

13. sērus, -a, -um . . . . late

VERBS

14. bibō, bibere, bibī, bibitum . . I drink
15. edō, edere, ēdī, ēsum . . . . . I eat

ADVERBS

16. crās . . . . tomorrow
17. herī . . . . yesterday
18. hodiē . . . . today
19. mox . . . . soon
20. nunc . . . . now

Chant:

Fifth Declension Noun Endings

LATIN   ENGLISH

	SINGULAR	PLURAL		SINGULAR	PLURAL
NOM.	-ēs	-ēs		a, the *noun*	the *nouns*
GEN.	-ēī / -eī	-ērum		of the *noun*, the *noun's*	of the *nouns*, the *nouns'*
DAT.	-ēī / -eī	-ēbus		to, for the *noun*	to, for the *nouns*
ACC.	-em	-ēs		the *noun*	the *nouns*
ABL.	-ē	-ēbus		by, with, from the *noun*	by, with, from the *nouns*

Quotation:

Cunīculus albus erat—"It was the white rabbit"

Weekly Worksheet 12

name: _____

A. Complete the chant for fifth declension nouns, then answer the questions.

	SINGULAR	PLURAL
NOM.		
GEN.		
DAT.		
ACC.		
ABL.		

1. Which ending tells you a noun's declension? _____

2. The fifth declension genitive singular ending is either _____ or _____.

3. If a fifth declension noun's base ends in a *vowel,* its genitive and _____ singular

   endings will be _____.

4. If a fifth declension noun's base ends in a *consonant,* its genitive and _____ singular

   endings will be _____.

5. The gender of most fifth declension nouns is _____.

6. There are no fifth declension nouns that are _____ in gender.

B. For each noun, list its genitive singular form, gender (M, F, or N), declension (1, 2, 3, 3i, 4, or 5), and English translation.

	NOUN	GENITIVE	GENDER	DECLENSION	TRANSLATION
1.	spēs				
2.	hōrologium				
3.	cunīculus				

	NOUN	GENITIVE	GENDER	DECLENSION	TRANSLATION
4.	rēgīna				
5.	diēs				
6.	tempus				
7.	fidēs				
8.	rēs				
9.	rēx				
10.	effigiēs				

C. Decline *diēs* and *rēs* in the charts below.

	SINGULAR	PLURAL
NOM.	diēs	
GEN.		
DAT.		
ACC.		
ABL.		

	SINGULAR	PLURAL
	rēs	

D. Give a synopsis for each of the following verbs.

1. *edō* in the second person plural:_____

	LATIN	ENGLISH
PRESENT ACT.		
FUTURE ACT.		
IMPERFECT ACT.		

2. *bibō* in the third person singular: _____

	LATIN	ENGLISH
PRESENT ACT.		
FUTURE ACT.		
IMPERFECT ACT.		

E. Decline the phrase *a new hope* in Latin.

	SINGULAR	PLURAL
NOM.		
GEN.		
DAT.		
ACC.		
ABL.		

F. Underline the adjective that goes with the noun (watch the endings—the nouns could be nominative or accusative, singular or plural), and then translate the phrase.

NOUN	ADJECTIVE	TRANSLATION
1. tempus	longum / longus	_____
2. rēs	flāvae / flāvus	_____
3. dōnum	sērōs / sērum	_____
4. rēx	callidus / callidum	_____
5. cunīculī	fessī / fessōs	_____
6. effigiem	album / albam	_____
7. fidēs	novum / nova	_____
8. diēs	ūmidās / ūmidōs	_____

G. Answer the questions about this week's quotation.

   1. Translate *Cunīculus albus erat* into English: _____

   2. What is the person, number, and tense of *erat?* _____

   3. What is the case and number of *albus?* _____

   4. What is the case and number of *cunīculus?* _____

H. On the lines below, give the Latin word for each picture!

1. _____   2. _____   3. _____   4. _____

5. _____   6. _____   7. _____   8. _____

I. Each sentence is missing a Latin word. Complete the sentences by translating the words in parentheses into Latin. Then translate the entire sentence into English.

   1. Flāva puella (sees) _____ cunīculum album._____

   _____

2. Cunīculus portat et spectat (a watch) _____. _____

_____

3. Puella explōrābit, et edet et bibet (small things) _____ _____ . _____

_____

4. Vidēbit (a magical cat) _____ et mīrōs flōrēs. _____

_____

5. Clāra (red queen) _____ _____ et quiēta alba rēgīna regnābunt. _____

_____

J. Translate these sentences into English.

1. Diēs mox erunt longī et gelidī. _____

2. Rēx erat sērus et currēbat. _____

3. Effigiēm laudābātis, sed nōn est bona. _____

_____

4. Oppidum herī oppugnābāmus; exercitum hodiē cavēbimus. _____

_____

5. Dōnum erat hōrologium novum et sumptuōsum. _____

_____

6. Tempus est merīdiēs et cēnam mox edam. _____

_____

7. Rēx rogat, "Dasne spem? Laudāsne fidem?" _____

_____

Translate these sentences into Latin.

8. The good king and the happy queen will drink wine and eat bread, cheese, and bacon. _____

_____

_____

9. Are you (sg.) able to see the clock now? _____

10. Yesterday I only was watching birds and things. _____

_____

K. Give a derivative for each of the following words.

1. spēs _____   3. tempus _____

2. diēs _____   4. rēs _____

WEEK 13

Word List

NOUNS

1. argūmentum, -ī (n) . . . . proof, evidence

2. auctōritās, auctōritātis (f) . . authority, influence, power

3. dēlictum, -ī (n) . . . . crime, sin, wrong

4. faciēs, faciēī (f) . . . . shape, form, figure, face

5. glaciēs, glaciēī (f) . . . . ice

6. iūdex, iūdicis (m) . . . . judge, juror

7. latrō, latrōnis (m) . . . . gangster, robber, highwayman

8. perniciēs, perniciēī (f) . . . . disaster, destruction

9. reus, -ī (m) . . . . defendant

10. sententia, -ae (f) . . . . . . opinion, decision

11. testimōnium, -ī (n) . . . . . testimony

ADJECTIVES

13. ignārus, -a, -um . . . . ignorant

14. iūstus, -a, -um . . . . just, right, fair, impartial

15. sevērus, -a, -um . . . . severe, strict, rigid

VERBS

16. conciliō (1) . . . . I win over, unite

17. conservō (1) . . . . I save, preserve

18. damnō (1) . . . . I condemn

19. iūrō (1) . . . . I swear, take an oath

20. peccō (1) . . . . I sin

Chant:

No new chant this week.

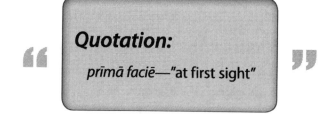

Quotation:

prīmā faciē—"at first sight"

Weekly Worksheet 13

name:

A. Complete the chant for fifth declension nouns.

	SINGULAR	PLURAL
NOM.		
GEN.		
DAT.		
ACC.		
ABL.		

B. Give the stem of each noun.

1. perniciēs _____

2. dēlictum _____

3. sententia _____

4. glaciēs _____

5. rēs _____

6. faciēs _____

7. iūdex _____

8. fidēs _____

C. Label each noun's declension (1, 2, 3, 3i, 4, or 5) and gender (M, F, or N). Then decline it. Do as much as possible from memory!

DECLENSION _____ GENDER _____

	SINGULAR	PLURAL
NOM.	faciēs	
GEN.		
DAT.		
ACC.		
ABL.		

DECLENSION _____ GENDER _____

	SINGULAR	PLURAL
NOM.	auctōritās	
GEN.		
DAT.		
ACC.		
ABL.		

DECLENSION _____ GENDER _____

	SINGULAR	PLURAL
NOM.	reus	
GEN.		
DAT.		
ACC.		
ABL.		

DECLENSION _____ GENDER _____

	SINGULAR	PLURAL
NOM.	glaciēs	
GEN.		
DAT.		
ACC.		
ABL.		

DECLENSION _____ GENDER _____

	SINGULAR	PLURAL
NOM.	perniciēs	
GEN.		
DAT.		
ACC.		
ABL.		

DECLENSION _____ GENDER _____

	SINGULAR	PLURAL
NOM.	dēlictum	
GEN.		
DAT.		
ACC.		
ABL.		

DECLENSION _____ GENDER _____

	SINGULAR	PLURAL
NOM.	pānis	
GEN.		
DAT.		
ACC.		
ABL.		

DECLENSION _____ GENDER _____

	SINGULAR	PLURAL
NOM.	sententia	
GEN.		
DAT.		
ACC.		
ABL.		

D. For each adjective, give the masculine, feminine, and neuter *accusative singular* forms in Latin.

	ADJECTIVE	MASCULINE	FEMININE	NEUTER
1.	ignorant			
2.	strict			
3.	fair			

E. Underline the adjective that goes with the noun (watch those endings!), and then translate the phrase.

NOUN	ADJECTIVE	TRANSLATION
1. latrōnem	sevērum / sevērus	_____
2. glaciēs	gelida / gelidus	_____
3. sententiās	sēram / sērās	_____
4. iūdicēs	iūstī / iūstās	_____
5. testimōnium	longa / longum	_____
6. perniciēs	cita / citus	_____
7. faciēs	rubrae / rubrī	_____
8. auctōritās	horrenda / horrendās	_____

F. Give a synopsis for each of the following verbs.

1. *iūrō* in the third person plural: _____

	LATIN	ENGLISH
PRESENT ACT.		
FUTURE ACT.		
IMPERFECT ACT.		

115

2. *conservō* in the first person singular: _____

_____

	LATIN	ENGLISH
PRESENT ACT.		
FUTURE ACT.		
IMPERFECT ACT.		

G. Fill in the principal parts.

1. conciliō, _____, _____, _____

2. peccō, _____, _____, _____

3. damnō, _____, _____, _____

H. Answer the questions about this week's quotation.

1. What does *prīmā faciē* mean in English? _____

2. What are the gender, number, and case of *faciē?* _____

I. Fill in the blanks.

1. The fifth declension genitive singular ending is either _____ or _____.

2. If a fifth declension noun's base ends in a *vowel,* its _____ and _____

    singular endings will be _____.

3. If a fifth declension noun's base ends in a *consonant,* its _____ and

    _____ singular endings will be _____.

4. The gender of almost all fifth declension nouns is _____.

J. Translate these sentences into English.

1. Reus ignārus iūdicem sevērum nōn conciliābit. _____

_____

2. Iūdicēs ignārī rēgīnam bonam hodiē damnant. _____

_____

3. Potesne reum conservāre? _____

4. Puella est sēra, sed testimōnium dabit. _____

_____

5. Rēx bonus et iūstus oppidum ignārum conservābit. _____

_____

6. Dēlictum est magnum, et poena erit sevēra. _____

_____

7. Vītāte perniciēm! _____

8. Peccāmus, sed Iūdex magnus et mīrus conservābit. _____

_____

9. Latrō canem calcitrat, sed canis latrōnem mordēbit! _____

_____

10. Iūdex lardum amat, et latrō iūdicem emere potest. _____

_____

Translate these sentences into Latin.

11. The evil robbers were taking oaths. _____

12. Yesterday, a dark figure was running. _____

13. The defendant is a clever gangster. _____

14. The judge was watching the trembling defendant. _____

_____

15. Was the ice evidence? _____

K. Match each derivative to its Latin root.

1. face   ignārus

2. ignore   conciliō

3. larceny   faciēs

4. reconcile   iūrō

5. perjury   latrō

WEEK 14

Word List

NOUNS

1. adulēscēns, adulēscēntis (m/f) . . . young man, young woman, young person
2. brācchium, -ī (n) . . . . arm
3. crūs, crūris (n) . . . . leg
4. medicīna, -ae (f) . . . . medicine
5. medicus, -ī (m) . . . . doctor, dentist
6. mulier, mulieris (f) . . . . woman
7. populus, -ī (m) . . . . people, nation
8. socius, -ī (m) . . . . companion, associate, ally
9. vir, virī (m) . . . . man
10. virgō, virginis (f) . . . . young woman, maiden

ADJECTIVES

11. acerbus, -a, -um . . . . bitter, harsh, painful
12. firmus, -a, -um . . . . firm, strong, healthy
13. grātus, -a, -um . . . . grateful, pleasing, agreeable
14. īrātus, -a, -um . . . . angry

ADVERBS

15. celeriter . . . . quickly, swiftly

VERBS

16. compleō, complēre, complēvī, complētum . . I fill, fill up
17. frangō, frangere, frēgī, fractum . . . . I break, smash, shatter
18. purgō (1) . . . . I clean, cleanse, clear
19. reparō (1) . . . . I fix, repair, restore
20. vulnerō (1) . . . . I wound

Chants:

Personal Pronouns

Ego, nōs: *I, we*

LATIN				ENGLISH	

	SINGULAR	PLURAL		SINGULAR	PLURAL
NOM.	ego	nōs		I	we
GEN.	meī	nostrum		of me	of us
DAT.	mihi	nōbīs		to, for me	to, for us
ACC.	mē	nōs		me	us
ABL.	mē	nōbīs		by, with, from me	by, with, from us

Tū, vōs: *you, you all*

LATIN				ENGLISH	

	SINGULAR	PLURAL		SINGULAR	PLURAL
NOM.	tū	vōs		you	you all
GEN.	tuī	vestrum		of you	of you all
DAT.	tibi	vōbīs		to, for you	to, for you all
ACC.	tē	vōs		you	you all
ABL.	tē	vōbīs		by, with, from you	by, with, from you all

Quotation:

Vēritās vōs līberābit—"The truth will set you (all) free"

Weekly Worksheet 14

name:

A. Decline these personal pronouns.

LATIN

	SINGULAR	PLURAL
NOM.	ego	
GEN.		
DAT.		nōbīs
ACC.		
ABL.		

ENGLISH

	SINGULAR	PLURAL
NOM.		
GEN.	of me	of us
DAT.	to, for me	to, for us
ACC.		
ABL.	by, with, from me	by, with, from us

	SINGULAR	PLURAL
NOM.		
GEN.		vestrum
DAT.		
ACC.		
ABL.	tē	

	SINGULAR	PLURAL
NOM.		
GEN.	of you	of you all
DAT.	to, for you	to, for you all
ACC.		
ABL.	by, with, from you	by, with, from you all

Now go back and circle all of the nominative and accusative Latin forms.

B. Fill in the blanks.

1. A noun names a _____, _____, or _____.

2. A pronoun takes the place of a _____.

3. The first person pronouns are _____ (singular) and _____ (plural).

4. The second person pronouns are _____ (singular) and _____ (plural).

5. The nominative forms of _____, nōs, _____, and _____ are

used only for emphasis.

C. Fill in the principal parts.

1. reparō, _____, _____, _____

2. conciliō, _____, _____, _____

3. vulnerō, _____, _____, _____

D. Give a synopsis for each of the following verbs.

1. *compleō* in the first person plural: _____

	LATIN	ENGLISH
PRESENT ACT.		
FUTURE ACT.		
IMPERFECT ACT.		

2. *purgō* in the second person singular: _____

	LATIN	ENGLISH
PRESENT ACT.		
FUTURE ACT.		
IMPERFECT ACT.		

3. *frangō* in the third person plural: _____

	LATIN	ENGLISH
PRESENT ACT.		
FUTURE ACT.		
IMPERFECT ACT.		

E. Answer the questions about this week's quotation.

1. What does *Vēritās vōs līberābit* mean in English? _____

2. Who originally said this? _____

3. What is the person, number, and case of *vōs*? _____

F. Complete the endings for each declension.

FIRST DECLENSION

	SINGULAR	PLURAL
NOM.		
GEN.		
DAT.		
ACC.		
ABL.		

SECOND DECLENSION

	SINGULAR	PLURAL
NOM.		
GEN.		
DAT.		
ACC.		
ABL.		

SECOND DECLENSION NEUTER

	SINGULAR	PLURAL
NOM.		
GEN.		
DAT.		
ACC.		
ABL.		

THIRD DECLENSION

	SINGULAR	PLURAL
NOM.		
GEN.		
DAT.		
ACC.		
ABL.		

THIRD DECLENSION NEUTER

	SINGULAR	PLURAL
NOM.		
GEN.		
DAT.		
ACC.		
ABL.		

THIRD DECLENSION I-STEM

	SINGULAR	PLURAL
NOM.		
GEN.		
DAT.		
ACC.		
ABL.		

THIRD DECLENSION NEUTER I-STEM

	SINGULAR	PLURAL
NOM.		
GEN.		
DAT.		
ACC.		
ABL.		

FOURTH DECLENSION

	SINGULAR	PLURAL
NOM.		
GEN.		
DAT.		
ACC.		
ABL.		

FOURTH DECLENSION NEUTER

	SINGULAR	PLURAL
NOM.		
GEN.		
DAT.		
ACC.		
ABL.		

FIFTH DECLENSION

	SINGULAR	PLURAL
NOM.		
GEN.		
DAT.		
ACC.		
ABL.		

G. Give the stem of each noun and the declension it's in (1, 2, 3, 3i, 4, or 5).

1. virgō _____

2. brācchium _____

3. vir _____

4. mulier _____

5. medicus _____

6. crūs _____

7. populus _____

8. socius _____

9. adulēscēns _____

10. medicīna _____

H. Underline the adjective that goes with the noun (watch those endings!), and then translate the phrase.

NOUN	ADJECTIVE	TRANSLATION
1. virgō	īrātus / īrāta	_____
2. populum	grātum / grātus	_____
3. medicīna	acerba / acerbus	_____
4. adulēscēns	firmum / firmus	_____
5. vir	cūriōsus / cūriōsī	_____
6. mulierēs	iūstī / iūstae	_____

7. crūs   magnus / magnum   _____

8. brācchia   gelida / gelidā   _____

I. Translate these sentences into English.

1. Medicus tē nunc vidēbit. _____

2. Adulēscēns dentem acerbum habet et rēs gelidās bibere nōn potest. _____

_____

3. Potestne medicus dentem malum complēre? _____

_____

4. Frange crūs! _____

5. Argūmentum firmum vōs conciliābit. _____

_____

6. Oppugnābitne canis magnus et firmus nōs? _____

_____

7. Medicus et socius dentēs flavōs celeriter purgant. _____

_____

8. Vōs nōn videō! _____

9. Virī īrātī nōs vulnerābant. _____

10. Vīnum est rubrum, mare est caeruleum, lac est album, et tē amō. _____

_____

Translate these sentences into Latin.

11. The people will condemn you all. _____

12. Save (sg.) me! _____

13. The medicine is bitter, but it will restore the grateful woman. _____

_____

14. The young woman clears the table. _____

15. I am not able to carry you! _____

J. Find and circle the hidden vocabulary words!

te	mulier	acerbus	vir	ego	populus
vulnero	crus	gratus	medicina	compleo	bracchium
celeriter	socius	vos	virgo	nos	reparo

```
A C E R B U S E D Y N X A V
R E B Y E Z O K A I O C M O
M L R U T G R A T U S E U S
I E A C O M P L E O T A S M
E R C M P O P U L U S A R R
T I C W Y U M E D I C I N A
L T H R E V U D E C R M Z I
O E I N G O L O S D U E V O
M R U S O C I U S I S L V R
U B M A B I E N E T E N I E
V I R G O M R I W L S A R P
E W T V U L N E R O C I N L
R E P A R O N T E M L O T P
```

WEEK 15

Word List

NOUNS

1. carcer, carceris (m) . . . . prison, jail

2. cīvis, cīvis (m/f) . . . . citizen

3. classis, classis (f) . . . . fleet (of ships)

4. dux, ducis (m). . . . . leader, guide, general

5. fābula, -ae (f) . . . . story, legend, fable

6. lītus, lītoris (n). . . . . shore, beach

7. misericordia, -ae (f) . . . . . pity, mercy

8. nāvis, nāvis (f). . . . . ship

9. perīculum, -ī (n). . . . . danger

10. pīrāta, -ae (m) . . . . pirate

11. proelium, -ī (n). . . . . battle, fight

12. psittacus, -ī (m) . . . . parrot

ADJECTIVES

13. aeger, aegra, aegrum . . . . sick, feeble

14. asper, aspera, asperum . . . rough, harsh

15. prīmus, -a, -um . . . . first, foremost

16. salvus, -a, -um. . . . . safe, secure, uninjured

VERBS

17. dīcō, dīcere, dīxī, dīctum . . . . I say, speak, tell, mention

18. gubernō (1) . . . . I pilot, steer, govern

19. lateō, latēre, latuī, —. . . . . I lie hidden, lurk, am concealed

20. nō, nāre, nāvī, —. . . . . I swim

Chant:

No new chant this week.

Quotation:

Deus gubernat nāvem—"God pilots the ship"

Weekly Worksheet 15
name:

A. Give a synopsis for each of the following verbs.

1. *nō* in the third person singular:_____

	LATIN	ENGLISH
PRESENT ACT.		
FUTURE ACT.		
IMPERFECT ACT.		

2. *dīcō* in the first person plural: _____

	LATIN	ENGLISH
PRESENT ACT.		
FUTURE ACT.		
IMPERFECT ACT.		

3. *lateō* in the second person plural: _____

	LATIN	ENGLISH
PRESENT ACT.		
FUTURE ACT.		
IMPERFECT ACT.		

B. Fill in the principal parts. In the parentheses at the end of the line, write which conjugation each verb is in (1, 2, or 3).

1. gubernō, _____, _____, _____ (_____)

2. frangō, _____, _____, _____ (_____)

3. caveō, _____, _____, _____ (_____)

4. spectō, _____, _____, _____ (_____)

C. Fill in the blanks.

1. A _____ names a person, _____, or thing.

2. A _____ takes the place of a noun.

3. The _____ _____ pronouns are *ego* (singular) and *nōs* (plural).

4. The _____ _____ pronouns are *tū* (singular) and *vōs* (plural).

5. The nominative forms of _____, _____, _____, and *vōs* are

used only for emphasis.

D. Decline these personal pronouns.

LATIN

	SINGULAR	PLURAL
NOM.	ego	nōs
GEN.		
DAT.		
ACC.		
ABL.		

ENGLISH

	SINGULAR	PLURAL
NOM.		
GEN.	of me	of us
DAT.	to, for me	to, for us
ACC.		
ABL.	by, with, from me	by, with, from us

	SINGULAR	PLURAL
NOM.	tū	vōs
GEN.		
DAT.		
ACC.		
ABL.		

	SINGULAR	PLURAL
NOM.		
GEN.	of you	of you all
DAT.	to, for you	to, for you all
ACC.		
ABL.	by, with, from you	by, with, from you all

E. Answer the questions about this week's quotation.

    1. What does *Deus gubernat nāvem* mean in English? _____

    2. What is the gender, number, and case of *nāvem?* _____

    3. What is the person, number, and tense of *gubernat?*_____

F. Give the genitive singular form, gender (M, F, or N), declension (1, 2, 3, 3i, 4, or 5), and the English translation for each Latin noun.

	NOUN	GENITIVE	GENDER	DECLENSION	TRANSLATION
1.	nāvis				
2.	pīrāta				
3.	classis				
4.	carcer				
5.	lītus				
6.	dux				
7.	insula				
8.	psittacus				
9.	perīculum				
10.	proelium				

G. Answer the following questions about derivatives from this week's Word List. The derivatives are italicized.

    1. The English word *peril* comes from the Latin word _____.

    2. If a journey is full of *perils,* that means it is full of _____.

    3. The English word *incarceration* comes from the Latin word _____.

    4. *Incarceration* is when someone is put in _____.

5. The English word *primer* comes from the Latin word _____.

6. A Latin *primer* is a book you use to learn your _____ things about Latin.

7. The English word *govern* comes from the Latin word _____.

8. When a mayor *governs* a town, he is _____ the town in a good direction.

H. Label each noun's declension (1, 2, 3, 3i, 4, or 5) and gender (M, F, or N). Then decline it. Do as much as possible from memory!

DECLENSION _____ GENDER _____

	SINGULAR	PLURAL
NOM.	cīvis	
GEN.		
DAT.		
ACC.		
ABL.		

DECLENSION _____ GENDER _____

	SINGULAR	PLURAL
NOM.	lītus	

I. Turn each verb into a singular command and a plural command in Latin. Then translate the plural command into English.

	VERB	SINGULAR COMMAND	PLURAL COMMAND	TRANSLATION
1.	dīcō			
2.	gubernō			
3.	lateō			
4.	nō			
5.	reparō			

J. Translate these sentences into English.

1. Cīvēs perīculum vident, sed nōn pugnābunt. _____

_____

2. Pīrātae malī classem oppugnant, et misericordiam nōn dēmonstrābunt. _____

_____

3. Proelium est ferum, et perīculum est magnum._____

_____

4. Psittacus ruber nāre nōn potest et dīcit, "Conservā mē!" _____

_____

5. Pīrāta asper ducem vulnerat et nāvem mox gubernat. _____

_____

6. Pīrāta acerbus nōs oppugnat et dīcit, "Crūra frangam! Brācchia frangam!" _____

_____

7. Pergentne pīrātae regnāre maria?_____

8. Iūdex firmus spectābat et exercitum celeriter convocat. _____

_____

9. Exercitus classem conservat, sed pīrātae poenam merēnt. _____

_____

10. Carcer est poena!_____

Translate these sentences into Latin.

11. The first story was long and bitter. _____

12. Are you sick? _____

13. Danger was lurking, but I am safe! _____

_____

14. The angry pirate says, "Swim (sg.) the river!" _____

_____

15. I will not wound you._____

WEEK 16

Word List

NOUNS

1. gurges, gurgitis (m) . . . . . . whirlpool, eddy, gulf

2. ignis, ignis (m) . . . . fire

3. insula, -ae (f) . . . . island

4. lignum, -ī (n) . . . . wood, timber, firewood

5. pars, partis (f) . . . . part, piece

ADJECTIVES

6. calidus, -a, -um . . . . warm, hot

VERBS

7. incendō, incendere, incendī, incensum . . . I kindle, set on fire

8. legō, legere, lēgī, lectum . . . . I gather, pick, read

Chant:

No new chant this week.

Quotation:

No new quotation this week.

Weekly Worksheet 16

name:

A. Complete the endings for each declension, then answer the questions.

FIRST DECLENSION

	SINGULAR	PLURAL
NOM.		
GEN.		
DAT.		
ACC.		
ABL.		

SECOND DECLENSION

	SINGULAR	PLURAL
NOM.		
GEN.		
DAT.		
ACC.		
ABL.		

SECOND DECLENSION NEUTER

	SINGULAR	PLURAL
NOM.		
GEN.		
DAT.		
ACC.		
ABL.		

THIRD DECLENSION

	SINGULAR	PLURAL
NOM.		
GEN.		
DAT.		
ACC.		
ABL.		

THIRD DECLENSION NEUTER

	SINGULAR	PLURAL
NOM.		
GEN.		
DAT.		
ACC.		
ABL.		

THIRD DECLENSION I-STEM

	SINGULAR	PLURAL
NOM.		
GEN.		
DAT.		
ACC.		
ABL.		

THIRD DECLENSION NEUTER I-STEM

	SINGULAR	PLURAL
NOM.		
GEN.		
DAT.		
ACC.		
ABL.		

FOURTH DECLENSION

	SINGULAR	PLURAL
NOM.		
GEN.		
DAT.		
ACC.		
ABL.		

FOURTH DECLENSION NEUTER

	SINGULAR	PLURAL
NOM.		
GEN.		
DAT.		
ACC.		
ABL.		

FIFTH DECLENSION

	SINGULAR	PLURAL
NOM.		
GEN.		
DAT.		
ACC.		
ABL.		

1. The fifth declension genitive singular ending is either _____ or _____.

2. If a fifth declension noun's base ends in a *vowel,* its genitive and _____ singular

    endings will be _____.

3. If a fifth declension noun's base ends in a *consonant,* its genitive and _____ singular

    endings will be _____.

B. Complete the third declension i-stem questions.

1. Does the noun's nominative singular end in _____ or _____ *and* have the

    _____ number of _____ in the nominative and _____

    singular? If so, then it is an i-stem.

2. Does the noun's nominative singular end in _____ or _____ *and* have a base ending in

    _____ _____? If so, then it is an i-stem.

3. Does the _____ noun's nominative singular end in _____, _____, or

    _____? If so, then it is a _____ i-stem.

C. Using the i-stem questions, tell whether each of the following nouns is an i-stem (Yes or No), and if it is, which question tells you so (1, 2, or 3).

1. gurges, gurgitis _____   6. cīvis, cīvis _____

2. ignis, ignis _____   7. lītus, lītoris _____

3. animal, animālis_____   8. pars, partis_____

4. nāvis, nāvis _____   9. classis, classis _____

5. adulēscēns, adulēscēntis_____   10. mare, maris _____

D. Fill in the principal parts. In the parentheses at the end of the line, write which conjugation each verb is in (1, 2, or 3).

1. incendō, _____, _____, _____ (_____)

2. _____, nāvigāre, _____, _____ (_____)

3. _____, _____, dīxī, _____ (_____)

4. legō, _____, _____, _____ (_____)

5. bibō, _____, _____, _____ (_____)

6. _____, _____, purgāvī, _____ (_____)

7. dō, _____, _____, _____ (_____)

8. conciliō, _____, _____, _____ (_____)

9. _____, mordēre, _____, _____ (_____)

10. _____, calcitrāre, _____, _____ (_____)

11. _____, _____, _____, ēsum (_____)

12. nō, _____, _____, _____ (_____)

E. Translate the Latin words into English, and the English words into Latin.

1. psittacus _____

2. animal _____

3. ratis _____

4. cāseus _____

5. effigiēs _____

6. quickly _____

7. blond _____

8. cēna _____

9. rēte _____

10. noon _____

11. macula _____

12. ignis _____

13. I was erring _____

14. favorite _____

15. rogō _____

16. distant _____

17. antrum _____

18. late _____

19. today _____

20. lignum _____

21. lītus _____

22. latrō _____

23. power _____

24. salvus _____

25. paene _____

26. they take an oath _____

27. squāma _____

28. socius _____

29. but _____

30. jail _____

F. Fill in the blanks, then complete the personal pronoun chants.

1. A pronoun takes the place of a _____.

2. The first person nominative pronouns are _____ (singular) and _____ (plural).

3. The second person nominative pronouns are _____ (singular) and _____ (plural).

LATIN

	SINGULAR	PLURAL
NOM.	ego	
GEN.		
DAT.		nōbīs
ACC.		
ABL.		

ENGLISH

	SINGULAR	PLURAL
GEN.	of me	of us
DAT.	to, for me	to, for us
ABL.	by, with, from me	by, with, from us

	SINGULAR	PLURAL
NOM.		
GEN.		
DAT.	tibi	vōbīs
ACC.		
ABL.		

	SINGULAR	PLURAL
GEN.	of you	of you all
DAT.	to, for you	to, for you all
ABL.	by, with, from you	by, with, from you all

G. Complete the Latin quotations, then give the English meaning of each.

1. Deōrum _____ est: _____

2. Hīc sunt _____: _____

3. Vēritās _____ _____: _____

_____

4. _____ canem: _____

5. _____ albus erat: _____

H. Label each noun's declension (1, 2, 3, 3i, 4, or 5) and gender (M, F, or N). Then decline it. Do as much as possible from memory!

DECLENSION _____ GENDER _____

	SINGULAR	PLURAL
NOM.	ignis	
GEN.		
DAT.		
ACC.		
ABL.		

DECLENSION _____ GENDER _____

	SINGULAR	PLURAL
NOM.	mare	

DECLENSION _____ GENDER _____

	SINGULAR	PLURAL
NOM.	faciēs	
GEN.		
DAT.		
ACC.		
ABL.		

DECLENSION _____ GENDER _____

	SINGULAR	PLURAL
NOM.	pars	

I. On the lines below, give the Latin word for each animal.

1. _____ 2. _____ 3. _____ 4. _____

5. _____   6. _____   7. _____   8. _____

J. Translate these sentences into English.

1. Incola ligna legit, et socius ignem celeriter incendit. _____

_____

2. Ignis est calidus, sed gurges est gelidus. _____

_____

3. Da partem. _____

4. Dracō est aeger et nōs nōn edet. _____

5. Diēs erat calidus, et mulierēs rēs gelidās bibēbant. _____

_____

6. Amantne monocerōtēs mare? _____

7. Avēs callidae fēlem magnam brūnam spectābunt. _____

_____

8. Rēx grātus mē laudābat, sed rēgīna īrāta vōs damnat. _____

_____

9. Reus argūmentum et testimōnia bona leget. _____

_____

10. Insula obscūra errat et mutat tempus. _____

_____

Translate these sentences into Latin.

11. The first fleet was only attacking pirates. _____

_____

12. The young woman almost wounded the dentist yesterday. _____

_____

13. Clean (pl.) the tables. _____

14. Are you almost able to swim? _____

15. Are the gangsters able to win over the strict judge? _____

_____

K. Match each derivative to its Latin root.

1. gurgle   dīcō

2. classic   medicus

3. peninsula   legō

4. diction   gurges

5. legible   pars

6. paramedic   avis

7. aviary   classis

8. part   insula

[This page intentionally blank]

3 UNIT THREE

UNIT 3: GOALS

Weeks 17–24

By the end of Unit 3, you should be able to . . .

- Recognize and distinguish third conjugation *-iō* and fourth conjugation verbs
- Chant from memory the perfect verb ending chants
- Give the principal parts for any verb from the Word Lists
- Give a verb synopsis including the present, future, imperfect, and perfect tenses
- Recognize, translate, and compose using nouns from any declension in the dative case

WEEK 17

Word List

NOUNS

1. auris, auris (f) . . . . ear
2. cursus, -ūs (m) . . . . race
3. laus, laudis (f) . . . . praise
4. mēta, -ae (f) . . . . goal, turning point, limit
5. testūdō, testūdinis (f) . . . . tortoise
6. vestīgium, vestīgiī (n) . . . . footprint, trace, track
7. victor, victōris (m) . . . . . . victor, winner
8. vulpēs, vulpis (f) . . . . fox

ADJECTIVES

9. tardus, -a, -um . . . . slow

ADVERBS

10. numquam . . . . never
11. simul . . . . at the same time
12. tardē . . . . slowly

VERBS

13. ambulō (1) . . . . I walk
14. audiō, audīre, audīvī, audītum . . . . I hear
15. dormiō, dormīre, dormīvī, dormītum . . . I sleep
16. inveniō, invenīre, invēnī, inventum . . . . . I find, discover, come upon
17. saliō, salīre, saluī, saltum . . . . I jump, leap, skip
18. surgō, surgere, surrēxī, surrēctum . . . . . I get up, rise
19. vincō, vincere, vīcī, victum . . . . I defeat, beat, conquer

Chants:

Present Active of *Audiō,* Fourth Conjugation Verb

LATIN

ENGLISH

	SINGULAR	PLURAL		SINGULAR	PLURAL
1ST	audiō	audīmus		I hear	we hear
2ND	audīs	audītis		you hear	you all hear
3RD	audit	audiunt		he/she/it hears	they hear

Future Active of *Audiō*

LATIN

ENGLISH

	SINGULAR	PLURAL		SINGULAR	PLURAL
1ST	audiam	audiēmus		I will hear	we will hear
2ND	audiēs	audiētis		you will hear	you all will hear
3RD	audiet	audient		he/she/it will hear	they will hear

Imperfect Active of *Audiō*

LATIN

ENGLISH

	SINGULAR	PLURAL		SINGULAR	PLURAL
1ST	audiēbam	audiēbāmus		I was hearing	we were hearing
2ND	audiēbās	audiēbātis		you were hearing	you all were hearing
3RD	audiēbat	audiēbant		he/she/it was hearing	they were hearing

Quotation:

No new quotation this week.

Weekly Worksheet 17

name:

A. First, answer the questions. Then following the pattern of *audiō*, conjugate and translate *saliō* in the present, future, and imperfect tenses.

1. List the principal parts of *saliō*: _____

2. Which conjugation is *saliō* in? _____

3. Which family is it in? _____

4. How do you find the stem of *saliō*? _____

5. What is the stem of *saliō*? _____

Present

LATIN

	SINGULAR	PLURAL
1ST	saliō	
2ND		
3RD		

ENGLISH

SINGULAR	PLURAL

Future

LATIN

	SINGULAR	PLURAL
1ST		
2ND		
3RD		

ENGLISH

SINGULAR	PLURAL

Imperfect

LATIN

ENGLISH

	SINGULAR	PLURAL		SINGULAR	PLURAL
1ST					
2ND					
3RD					

B. For each verb, fill in the principal parts and circle the stem. In the parentheses at the end of the line, write which conjugation each verb is in (1, 2, 3, or 4).

1. audiō, _____, _____, _____ (_____)

2. vincō, _____, _____, _____ (_____)

3. ambulō, _____, _____, _____ (_____)

C. Give a synopsis for each of the following verbs.

1. *dormiō* in the second person plural: _____

	LATIN	ENGLISH
PRESENT ACT.		
FUTURE ACT.		
IMPERFECT ACT.		

2. *surgō* in the third person singular: _____

	LATIN	ENGLISH
PRESENT ACT.		
FUTURE ACT.		
IMPERFECT ACT.		

3. *inveniō* in the first person singular:_____

	LATIN	ENGLISH
PRESENT ACT.		
FUTURE ACT.		
IMPERFECT ACT.		

D. Each sentence is missing a Latin word. Complete the sentences by translating the words in parentheses into Latin. Then translate the entire sentence into English.

1. Vulpēs currēbant et (were leaping) _____._____

_____

2. Tardus cīvis nōn amat (races) _____._____

_____

3. Auris (hears) _____ et ōs gustat. _____

_____

4. Potestne magna testūdō (to jump) _____? _____

_____

5. (I will sleep) _____ nunc et surgam crās. _____

_____

E. Decline *pointed ear.*

	SINGULAR	PLURAL
NOM.		
GEN.		
DAT.		
ACC.		
ABL.		

F. For each noun, give its genitive singular form, declension (1, 2, 3, 3i, 4, or 5), base, and translation.

	NOUN	GENITIVE	DECLEN.	BASE	TRANSLATION
1.	laus				
2.	cursus				
3.	victor				
4.	testūdō				
5.	mēta				
6.	vulpēs				
7.	vestīgium				

G. On the lines below, give the Latin word for each picture. If there is more than one, give the plural!

1. _____   2. _____   3. _____   4. _____

H. For each verb, give the person (1, 2, or 3), number (S or P), tense, and translation.

	VERB	PERSON	NUMBER	TENSE	TRANSLATION
1.	invenīmus				
2.	audiēs				
3.	ambulābant				
4.	salītis				
5.	vincet				
6.	audiam				
7.	dormiēbam				
8.	surgunt				

I. Translate these sentences into English.

1. Cunīculus citus cursum habēbit. _____

2. Cunīculus celeriter currit et salit, sed testūdō tardē ambulābit. _____

_____

3. Mox cunīculus est fessus, et dormiet. _____

_____

4. Simul testūdō fīda ambulāre pergit. _____

_____

5. Cunīculus sērus surgit, et clārās et longinquās laudēs audit. _____

_____

6. Vestīgia videt et dicit, "Vincitne testūdō mē?" _____

_____

7. Cunīculus mētam videt, sed testūdō est victor! _____

_____

8. Animālia testūdinem laudābunt, sed simul cunīculum amant. _____

_____

9. Cunīculus et testūdō rident et bibunt. _____

_____

10. Cursum novum mox current. _____

Translate these sentences into Latin.

11. I hear you, but I do not see you! _____

12. The giant tortoise was sleeping but will slowly get up. _____

_____

13. The grateful victors love and gather praises. _____

_____

14. The fox is never able to find the quiet quail (pl.). _____

_____

15. The clever guards will discover the hidden footprints. _____

_____

WEEK 18

Word List

NOUNS

1. agricola, -ae (m) . . . . farmer

2. arbor, arboris (f) . . . . tree

3. architectus, -ī (m). . . . . . . architect

4. comes, comitis (m). . . . . . companion, fellow-traveler

5. coquus, -ī (m) . . . . cook, chef

6. explōrātor, explōrātōris (m) . explorer, scout, guide

7. grāmen, grāminis (n) . . . . . grass, greenery

8. holus, holeris (n) . . . . vegetable

9. iūs, iūris (n). . . . . soup

10. ovis, ovis (f) . . . . sheep

11. pastor, pastōris (m) . . . . . shepherd

12. pōns, pōntis (m). . . . . . . bridge

13. scopulus, -ī (m) . . . . cliff, crag

VERBS

14. capiō, capere, cēpī, captum . . . . I take, receive, capture, catch

15. conveniō, convenīre, convēnī, conventum . . I meet together, come together

16. faciō, facere, fēcī, factum . . . . I make, do, build

17. fugiō, fugere, fūgī, fugitum . . . . I run away, flee

18. scandō, scandere, scandī, scansum . . . . . I climb

19. tussiō, tussīre, tussī, tussītum. . . . . I cough

CONJUNCTIONS/ADVERBS

20. vel . . . . or (conj.), even (adv.)

Chants:

Present Active of *Capiō*, Third Conjugation *-iō* Verb

LATIN

ENGLISH

	SINGULAR	PLURAL		SINGULAR	PLURAL
1ST	cap**iō**	cap**imus**		I take	we take
2ND	cap**is**	cap**itis**		you take	you all take
3RD	cap**it**	cap**iunt**		he/she/it takes	they take

Future Active of *Capiō*

LATIN

ENGLISH

	SINGULAR	PLURAL		SINGULAR	PLURAL
1ST	cap**iam**	cap**iēmus**		I will take	we will take
2ND	cap**iēs**	cap**iētis**		you will take	you all will take
3RD	cap**iet**	cap**ient**		he/she/it will take	they will take

Imperfect Active of *Capiō*

LATIN

ENGLISH

	SINGULAR	PLURAL		SINGULAR	PLURAL
1ST	cap**iēbam**	cap**iēbāmus**		I was taking	we were taking
2ND	cap**iēbās**	cap**iēbātis**		you were taking	you all were taking
3RD	cap**iēbat**	cap**iēbant**		he/she/it was taking	they were taking

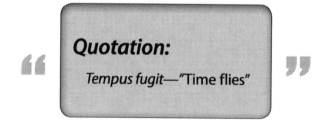

Quotation:

Tempus fugit—"Time flies"

Weekly Worksheet 18

name: _____

A. First, answer the questions. Then following the pattern of *capiō,* conjugate and translate *faciō* in present, future, and imperfect tenses.

1. List the principal parts of *faciō:* _____

2. Give the imperative forms (singular and plural) of *faciō:* _____

3. Which conjugation is *faciō* in? _____

4. Is it a third conjugation *-iō* verb? _____

5. How do you know? _____

_____

6. Do third conjugation *-iō* verbs conjugate more like the third conjugation or the fourth

conjugation? _____

Present

LATIN

	SINGULAR	PLURAL
1ST	faciō	
2ND		
3RD		

ENGLISH

	SINGULAR	PLURAL
1ST		
2ND		
3RD		

Future

LATIN

	SINGULAR	PLURAL
1ST		
2ND		
3RD		

ENGLISH

	SINGULAR	PLURAL
1ST		
2ND		
3RD		

ENGLISH

	PLURAL		SINGULAR	PLURAL

B. For each verb, fill in the principal parts and circle the stem. In the parentheses, write which conjugation each verb is in (1, 2, 3, 3io, or 4).

1. vincō, _____, _____, _____ (_____)

2. audiō, _____, _____, _____ (_____)

3. conveniō, _____, _____, _____ (_____)

C. Give a synopsis for each of the following verbs.

1. *fugiō* in the first person plural: _____

	LATIN	ENGLISH
PRESENT ACT.		
FUTURE ACT.		
IMPERFECT ACT.		

2. *tussiō* in the second person singular: _____

	LATIN	ENGLISH
PRESENT ACT.		
FUTURE ACT.		
IMPERFECT ACT.		

3. *scandō* in the third person plural: _____

	LATIN	ENGLISH
PRESENT ACT.		
FUTURE ACT.		
IMPERFECT ACT.		

4. *capiō* in the third person singular: _____

	LATIN	ENGLISH
PRESENT ACT.		
FUTURE ACT.		
IMPERFECT ACT.		

D. Each sentence is missing a Latin word. Complete the sentences by translating the words in parentheses into Latin. Then translate the entire sentence into English.

1. Pastor spectābit (the sheep, pl.) _____. _____

_____

2. Explōrātōrēs (were climbing) _____ scopulōs._____

_____

3. Architectus (will make) _____ magnum pōntem. _____

_____

4. Ferus canis (will not catch) _____ ovēs. _____

_____

5. Coquī (are gathering) _____ lactūcās et holera._____

_____

E. For each noun, give its genitive singular form, gender (M, F, or N), declension (1, 2, 3, 3i, 4, or 5), and translation.

	NOUN	GENITIVE	GENDER	DECLENSION	TRANSLATION
1.	arbor				
2.	comes				
3.	grāmen				
4.	holus				
5.	agricola				
6.	iūs				
7.	pōns				

F. On the lines below, give the Latin word for each picture.

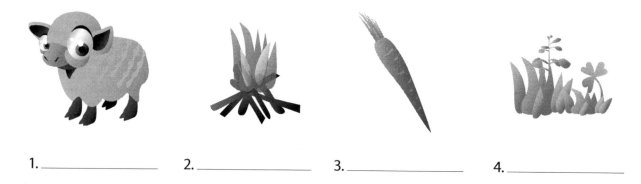

1. _____   2. _____   3. _____   4. _____

G. For each verb, give the person (1, 2, or 3), number (S or P), tense, conjugation (1, 2, 3, 3io, or 4), and translation.

	VERB	PERSON	NUMBER	CONJ.	TENSE	TRANSLATION
1.	fugiam					
2.	scandet					
3.	vincēbāmus					
4.	conveniēbātis					

	VERB	PERSON	NUMBER	CONJ.	TENSE	TRANSLATION
5.	salīs					
6.	facient					
7.	tussītis					
8.	capiunt					

H. Answer the questions about this week's quotation.

1. What does *Tempus fugit* mean in English? _____

2. What is the declension and gender of the noun? _____

3. What is the person, number, and case of the verb? _____

I. Translate these sentences into English.

1. Pastōrēs ovēs trepidās celeriter capient, vel ovēs fugient._____

_____

2. Explōrātor holera legit et iūs faciet. _____

_____

3. Architectus malus et index conveniunt, et carcerem horrendum facient._____

_____

4. Hostis oppugnat et exercitūs fugiunt. _____

_____

5. Capietne coquus īrātus canem callidam? _____

_____

6. Explōrātor nōs inveniet et conservābit! _____

7. Architectus nōn est perītus, et pōntem facere nōn potest. _____

_____

8. Vulpēs tarda testūdinēs sōlum capit. _____

9. Adulēscēns numquam erit pastor vel custōs. _____

10. Comes dicēbat, "Cape holera!" _____

_____

Translate these sentences into Latin.

11. The explorer will even climb the high crags. _____

_____

12. The men are new farmers. _____

13. The sick chef was cleaning dishes and coughing. _____

_____

14. Is the sheep black? _____

15. The guide and the fellow-travelers will meet together quickly._____

_____

I. Here are some derivatives from this week's Word List. Look up each word's definition (online or in a dictionary) and write it on the lines. In the parentheses, write each word's Latin root.

1. ovine: _____ (_____)

2. fugitive: _____ (_____)

3. pontoon: _____

_____ (_____)

WEEK 19

Word List

NOUNS

1. amīcus, -ī (m) . . . . friend
2. benevolentia, -ae (f). . . . . favor, good will
3. fāma, -ae (f) . . . . report, rumor
4. hospes, hospitis (m) . . . . . guest, host
5. labor, labōris (m) . . . . work, toil, hardship
6. līberī, līberōrum (m, pl.) . . . children
7. littera, -ae (f). . . . . letter (of the alphabet)
   plural: litterae, -ārum. . . . . letter (correspondence), letters (of the alphabet)
8. māter, mātris (f) . . . . mother
9. pater, patris (m). . . . . father

ADJECTIVES

10. multus, -a, -um . . . . much, many
11. pulcher, pulchra, pulchrum. . . . . beautiful, handsome

VERBS

12. accipiō, accipere, accēpī, acceptum . . . . . . I accept, receive
13. cupiō, cupere, cupīvī, cupītum . . . . I want, long for, wish for
14. narrō (1). . . . . I tell, relate, recount
15. recitō (1) . . . . I read aloud, recite
16. sciō, scīre, scīvī, scītum . . . . I know, understand
17. sentiō, sentīre, sensī, sensum. . . . . I feel, experience

CONJUNCTIONS

18. -que . . . . and

Chants:

No new chant this week.

Quotation:

Senātus Populusque Rōmānus (SPQR)—"The Senate and the People of Rome"

Weekly Worksheet 19

name: _____

A. Answer the following questions. Then conjugate *audiō* in the present, future, and imperfect tenses.

1. List the principal parts of *audiō:* _____

2. Which conjugation is *audiō* in? _____

3. How do you know? _____

Present

	SINGULAR	PLURAL
1ST		
2ND		
3RD		

Future

	SINGULAR	PLURAL
1ST		
2ND		
3RD		

Imperfect

	SINGULAR	PLURAL
1ST		
2ND		
3RD		

B. Answer the following questions. Then conjugate *capiō* in the present, future, and imperfect tenses.

1. List the principal parts of *capiō:* _____

2. Which conjugation is *capiō* in? _____

3. Is it a third conjugation *-iō* verb? _____

4. How do you know? _____

_____

5. Do third conjugation *-iō* verbs conjugate more like the third or the fourth conjugation?

_____

Present

	SINGULAR	PLURAL
1ST		
2ND		
3RD		

Future

	SINGULAR	PLURAL
1ST		
2ND		
3RD		

Imperfect

	SINGULAR	PLURAL
1ST		
2ND		
3RD		

C. Underline the adjective that goes with the subject noun and then translate the phrase. (Remember to watch the gender and case!)

NOUN	ADJECTIVE	TRANSLATION
1. māter	pulcher / pulchra / pulchrī	_____
2. agricolae	multus / multae / multī	_____
3. amīcus	cārus / cārum / cāra	_____
4. iūs	callidum / callidus / callida	_____
5. litterae	longa / longī / longae	_____
6. hospitēs	clārī / clārīs / clārae	_____
7. fāmam	mīrum / mīram / mīra	_____

D. Give a synopsis for each of the following verbs.

1. *narrō* in the third person singular: _____

	LATIN	ENGLISH
PRESENT ACT.		
FUTURE ACT.		
IMPERFECT ACT.		

2. *sciō* in the first person plural: _____

	LATIN	ENGLISH
PRESENT ACT.		
FUTURE ACT.		
IMPERFECT ACT.		

3. *cupiō* in the third person plural: _____

	LATIN	ENGLISH
PRESENT ACT.		
FUTURE ACT.		
IMPERFECT ACT.		

4. *sentiō* in the second person singular: _____

	LATIN	ENGLISH
PRESENT ACT.		
FUTURE ACT.		
IMPERFECT ACT.		

E. For each noun, give its genitive singular form, gender (M, F, or N), declension (1, 2, 3, 3i, 4, or 5), and translation.

	NOUN	GENITIVE	GENDER	DECLENSION	TRANSLATION
1.	littera				
2.	benevolentia				
3.	pater				
4.	hospes				
5.	labor				
6.	iūs				
7.	comes				
8.	fāma				
9.	amīcus				
10.	māter				

F. Label each noun's declension (1, 2, 3, 3i, 4, or 5) and gender (M, F, or N). Then decline it.

DECLENSION _____ GENDER _____   DECLENSION _____ GENDER _____

	SINGULAR	PLURAL
NOM.	ovis	
GEN.		
DAT.		
ACC.		
ABL.		

	SINGULAR	PLURAL
NOM.	holus	
GEN.		
DAT.		
ACC.		
ABL.		

G. Answer the questions about this week's quotation.

1. What does the Latin abbreviation SPQR stand for? _____

_____

2. What does the Q stand for? _____

3. Can -que be used on its own as a word? _____

4. Translate the phrase into English: _____

H. For each verb, give the person (1, 2, or 3), number (S or P), conjugation (1, 2, 3, 3io, or 4), tense, and translation.

	VERB	PERSON	NUMBER	CONJ.	TENSE	TRANSLATION
1.	accipiēs					
2.	recitātis					
3.	scient					
4.	cupiēbās					
5.	fugient					
6.	sentiam					

	VERB	PERSON	NUMBER	CONJ.	TENSE	TRANSLATION
7.	accipiēbat					
8.	capiunt					
9.	convenīmus					
10.	vincit					

I. Translate these sentences into English.

1. Arbor pulchra est firma celsaque. _____

2. Vir multās labōrēs sentiēbat, et misericordiam nōn cupiēbat. _____

_____

3. Habentne līberī malī multōs amīcōs? _____

4. Scīmus tē, sed scīsne nōs? _____

5. Pater vel māter fābulam recitābit. _____

_____

6. Multās fāmās celeriter beneque narrābās. _____

_____

7. Līberī raucī tussiēbant et medicīnam accipiēbant. _____

_____

8. Explōrātor salvus spem sentit, sed comes crūs acerbum habet. _____

_____

9. Architectus pōntēs aedificiaque parva sōlum facere cupit. _____

_____

10. Pater audāciam magnam habet et fugere numquam cupiet. _____

_____

Translate these sentences into Latin. Practice using *-que* wherever possible!

11. The angry guest does not feel good will. _____

12. The father and mother want many children. _____

_____

13. I will read the first letter aloud. _____

14. The girl was longing for a dog and a horse. _____

15. A happy sheep will accept grass and flowers. _____

_____

J. Each sentence below uses a derivative (in italics). Use your knowledge of Latin to finish each sentence by circling the correct answer!

1. When someone is *amicable,* it means they are _____.

    a) curious   b) friendly   c) always talking   d) tired

2. Your *maternal* grandfather is your _____ father.

    a) brother's   b) mother's   c) father's   d) friend's

3. A *multitude* is a group of _____ people.

    a) funny   b) beautiful   c) famous   d) many

4. A *pulchritudinous* person is someone who is quite _____.

    a) odd   b) tall   c) beautiful   d) generous

WEEK 20

Word List

NOUNS

1. aqua, -ae (f) . . . . water
2. cavum, -ī (n) . . . . hole
3. ēricius, -ī (m) . . . . hedgehog
4. fungus, -ī (m) . . . . mushroom, fungus
5. imber, imbris (m) . . . . rain
6. līmus, -ī (m) . . . . mud
7. lūdus, -ī (m) . . . . game, play, school
8. mēlēs, mēlis (f) . . . . badger
9. nucleus, -ī (m) . . . . nut
10. sciūrus, -ī (m) . . . . squirrel
11. vermis, vermis (m) . . . . . . worm

ADJECTIVES

12. rīdiculus, -a, -um . . . . funny, amusing

VERBS

13. aperiō, aperīre, aperuī, apertum . . . I open
14. doceō, docēre, docuī, doctum . . . . . I teach
15. fodiō, fodere, fōdī, fossum . . . . I dig
16. iaciō, iacere, iēcī, iactum . . . . I throw
17. lūdō, lūdere, lūsī, lūsum . . . . I play
18. occultō (1) . . . . I hide

Chants:

Perfect Active Verb Endings

	LATIN			ENGLISH	
	SINGULAR	**PLURAL**		**SINGULAR**	**PLURAL**
1ST	-ī	-imus		I *verbed,* have *verbed*	we *verbed*
2ND	-istī	-istis		you *verbed*	you all *verbed*
3RD	-it	-ērunt		he/she/it *verbed*	they *verbed*

Examples of Verbs in the Perfect Tense

Perfect Active of *Amō,* First Conjugation Verb

	LATIN			ENGLISH	
	SINGULAR	**PLURAL**		**SINGULAR**	**PLURAL**
1ST	amāvī	amāvimus		I loved, have loved	we loved
2ND	amāvistī	amāvistis		you loved	you all loved
3RD	amāvit	amāvērunt		he/she/it loved	they loved

Perfect Active of *Videō,* Second Conjugation Verb

	LATIN			ENGLISH	
	SINGULAR	**PLURAL**		**SINGULAR**	**PLURAL**
1ST	vīdī	vīdimus		I saw, have seen	we saw
2ND	vīdistī	vīdistis		you saw	you all saw
3RD	vīdit	vīdērunt		he/she/it saw	they saw

Perfect Active of *Dūcō,* Third Conjugation Verb

	LATIN			ENGLISH	
	SINGULAR	**PLURAL**		**SINGULAR**	**PLURAL**
1ST	dūxī	dūximus		I led, have led	we led
2ND	dūxistī	dūxistis		you led	you all led
3RD	dūxit	dūxērunt		he/she/it led	they led

Perfect Active of *Audiō,* Fourth Conjugation Verb

LATIN

	SINGULAR	PLURAL
1ST	audīvī	audīvimus
2ND	audīvistī	audīvistis
3RD	audīvit	audīvērunt

ENGLISH

	SINGULAR	PLURAL
	I heard, have heard	we heard
	you heard	you all heard
	he/she/it heard	they heard

Perfect Active of *Capiō,* Third Conjugation *-iō* Verb

LATIN

	SINGULAR	PLURAL
1ST	cēpī	cēpimus
2ND	cēpistī	cēpistis
3RD	cēpit	cēpērunt

ENGLISH

	SINGULAR	PLURAL
	I took, have taken	we took
	you took	you all took
	he/she/it took	they took

> ## *Quotation:*
>
> *Vēnī, vīdī, vīcī*—"I came, I saw, I conquered"

[This page intentionally blank]

Weekly Worksheet 20   *name:*

A. In the boxes below, write perfect active verb ending chant. Then answer the questions.

	SINGULAR	PLURAL
1ST		
2ND		
3RD		

1. Which tense are these endings for? _____

2. Which stem do these endings attach to? _____

3. How do you find the perfect stem of a verb? _____

_____

4. Is this how you find the perfect stem for *all* conjugations? _____

B. Fill in the principal parts for each of the following verbs, and circle the perfect stem. In the parentheses at the end of the line, write which conjugation each verb is in (1, 2, 3, 3io, 4, or 5).

1. lūdō, _____, _____, _____ (_____)

2. compleō, _____, _____, _____ (_____)

3. recitō, _____, _____, _____ (_____)

4. legō, _____, _____, _____ (_____)

5. accipiō, _____, _____, _____ (_____)

6. sedeō, _____, _____, _____ (_____)

7. iaciō, _____, _____, _____ (_____)

8. caveō, _____, _____, _____ (_____)

9. ambulō, _____, _____, _____ (_____)

10. faciō, _____, _____, _____ (_____)

11. dīcō, _____, _____, _____ (_____)

12. inveniō, _____, _____, _____ (_____)

13. tussiō, _____, _____, _____ (_____)

14. mordeō, _____, _____, _____ (_____)

15. dō, _____, _____, _____ (_____)

C. The perfect tense can be translated several ways. Study the example given below, and then give three different possible translations for each of the following perfect verbs.

amāvī   *I loved, I have loved, I did love*

1. rogāvistis _____

2. narrāvimus_____

3. iēcistī _____

4. dīxit _____

5. ēdērunt _____

C. Conjugate and translate *lūdō* in the perfect tense.

LATIN   ENGLISH

	SINGULAR	PLURAL		SINGULAR	PLURAL
1ST					
2ND					
3RD					

D. Conjugate and translate *doceō* in the perfect tense.

LATIN   ENGLISH

	SINGULAR	PLURAL		SINGULAR	PLURAL
1ST					
2ND					
3RD					

E. Give a synopsis for each of the following verbs. When you write out the principal parts, circle the perfect stem.

1. *fodiō* in the third person plural: _____

	LATIN	ENGLISH
PRESENT ACT.		
FUTURE ACT.		
IMPERFECT ACT.		
PERFECT ACT.		

2. *aperiō* in the second person singular:_____

	LATIN	ENGLISH
PRESENT ACT.		
FUTURE ACT.		
IMPERFECT ACT.		
PERFECT ACT.		

3. *occultō* in the first person plural: _____

	LATIN	ENGLISH
PRESENT ACT.		
FUTURE ACT.		
IMPERFECT ACT.		
PERFECT ACT.		

4. *doceō* in the third person singular: _____

	LATIN	ENGLISH
PRESENT ACT.		
FUTURE ACT.		
IMPERFECT ACT.		
PERFECT ACT.		

F. For each noun, give its genitive singular form, gender (M, F, or N), declension (1, 2, 3, 3i, 4, or 5), and translation.

	NOUN	GENITIVE	GENDER	DECLENSION	TRANSLATION
1.	imber				
2.	ēricius				
3.	mēlēs				
4.	aqua				
5.	cavum				
6.	vermis				
7.	nucleus				
8.	lūdus				

	NOUN	GENITIVE	GENDER	DECLENSION	TRANSLATION
9.	līmus				
10.	sciūrus				

G. Answer the questions about this week's quotation.

1. What does *Vēnī, vīdī, vīcī* mean in English? _____

2. Who originally said this? _____

3. What is the person, number, and tense of *vīdī*? _____

4. *Vīcī* is the perfect tense of what Latin verb? _____

H. For each verb, give the person (1, 2, or 3), number (S or P), conjugation (1, 2, 3, 3io, or 4), tense, and translation.

	VERB	PERSON	NUMBER	CONJ.	TENSE	TRANSLATION
1.	scīvimus					
2.	cupit					
3.	dormīvistis					
4.	surrēxī					
5.	docēbātis					
6.	fēcit					
7.	lūditis					
8.	recitāvistī					
9.	aperiēmus					
10.	iēcit					

I. Each sentence is missing a Latin word. Complete the sentences by translating the words in parentheses into Latin. Then translate the entire sentence into English.

1. Exercitus (attacked) _____. _____

2. Ovēs (have wandered) _____. _____

3. Imber (filled up) _____ cavum. _____

4. Mēlēs rīdicula (threw) _____ līmum. _____

5. (Did you understand) _____ fāmam? _____

J. Translate these sentences into English.

1. Sciūrus ruber nucleum aperuit. _____

2. Vermēs līmum edere amāvērunt. _____

3. Mēlēs nigra multa cava fōdit. _____

4. Agricolae sociusque hodiē convēnērunt. _____

_____

5. Fāmam scīvī, sed fāmam nōn narrāvī. _____

_____

6. Vir grātus rīsit et labōrem bene fēcit. _____

_____

7. Cupīvitne canis mēlem mordēre? _____

8. Mulier rīdicula lūdōs lūsit et fābulās mīrās narrāvit. _____

_____

9. Ducēs dīxērunt, "Invēnimus indicem." _____

_____

10. Ēricius serpentem parvum et multōs fungōs ēdit. _____

_____

Translate these sentences into Latin.

11. I have not slept! _____

12. The angry squirrel threw nuts. _____

13. A dragon has taken and hidden the gold. _____

14. The faithful king deserved to rule. _____

15. Did you ever climb the mountain? _____

K. Each sentence below uses a derivative (in italics). Use your knowledge of Latin to finish each sentence by circling the correct answer!

1. To find a *fossil,* you must begin by _____ .

    a) eating   b) playing   c) hiding   d) digging

2. An *urchin* is a sea animal covered with spikes like a _____ .

    a) dragon   b) castle gate   c) hedgehog   d) pincushion

3. *Vermicelli* is a type of noodle that is long and thin like a _____ .

    a) worm   b) ruler   c) pencil   d) giraffe

[This page intentionally blank]

WEEK 21

Word List

NOUNS

1. aedīlis, aedīlis (m) . . . . sheriff, public officer

2. armentārius, -ī (m) . . . . cowboy, herdsman

3. fātum, -ī (n) . . . . fate, destiny

4. lex, lēgis (f) . . . . law

5. lupus, -ī (m) . . . . wolf

6. petasus, -ī (m) . . . . hat

7. proscrīptus, -ī (m) . . . . outlaw

8. sclopētum, -ī (n) . . . . gun

9. vastitās, vastitātis (f) . . . . . desert, emptiness, wilderness

10. vestis, vestis (f) . . . . clothing, garment

11. vultur, vulturis (m) . . . . . . vulture

ADJECTIVES

12. āridus, -a, -um . . . . dry

13. famēlicus, -a, -um . . . . . . hungry

14. pulvereus, -a, -um . . . . . . dusty

15. sōlus, -a, -um . . . . only, alone, lone

VERBS

16. clāmō (1) . . . . I shout

17. equitō (1) . . . . I ride (a horse), ride horseback

18. gerō, gerere, gessī, gestum . . . . I wear, bear

19. mittō, mittere, mīsī, missum . . . . . . I send

20. occidō, occidere, occidī, occāsum . . . I fall, fall down, die

Chants:

No new chant this week.

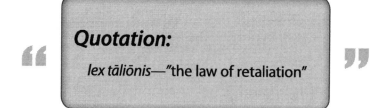

> **Quotation:**
>
> *lex tāliōnis*—"the law of retaliation"

Weekly Worksheet 21

name:

A. In the boxes below, write the verb endings for the perfect tense. Then answer the questions.

	SINGULAR	PLURAL
1ST		
2ND		
3RD		

1. Which stem do these endings attach to? _____

2. How do you form the perfect stem of any verb? _____

_____

B. Fill in the principal parts for each of the following verbs, and circle the perfect stem. In the parentheses at the end of the line, write which conjugation each verb is in (1, 2, 3, 3io, 4, or 5).

1. clāmō, _____, _____, _____ (____)

2. gerō, _____, _____, _____ (____)

3. mittō, _____, _____, _____ (____)

4. currō, _____, _____, _____ (____)

5. bibō, _____, _____, _____ (____)

6. occidō, _____, _____, _____ (____)

7. laudō, _____, _____, _____ (____)

8. equitō, _____, _____, _____ (____)

9. pugnō, _____, _____, _____ (____)

10. explōrō, _____, _____, _____ (____)

C. Give the person (1, 2, or 3), number (S or P), and tense of each English phrase, then translate it into Latin.

	ENGLISH	PERSON	NUMBER	TENSE	LATIN TRANSLATION
1.	you wore				
2.	I rode horseback				
3.	they shouted				
4.	we will send				
5.	it has died				
6.	you all drank				
7.	he was falling				
8.	we did explore				
9.	they ran				
10.	I am wearing				

D. The perfect tense can be translated several ways. Study the example given below, then give three different possible translations for each of the following perfect verbs.

dedistī   *you gave, you have given, you did give*

1. pugnāvērunt _____

2. mīsī _____

3. gessimus _____

4. equitāvit _____

5. clāmāvistis _____

6. docuistī _____

E. Decline the irregular adjective *sōlus* in the masculine. Remember, it declines just like *bonus*, except in the genitive and dative singular!

	SINGULAR	PLURAL
NOM.		
GEN.		
DAT.		
ACC.		
ABL.		

F. For each noun, give its base, gender (M, F, or N), declension (1, 2, 3, 3i, 4, or 5), and translation. Try to do as much as you can from memory!

	NOUN	BASE	GENDER	DECLENSION	TRANSLATION
1.	vultur				
2.	vestis				
3.	proscrīptus				
4.	lex				
5.	sclopētum				
6.	armentārius				
7.	fātum				
8.	petasus				
9.	aedīlis				
10.	aqua				
11.	lupus				
12.	vastitās				

G. Give a synopsis for each of the following verbs. When you write out the principal parts, circle the perfect stem.

1. *occidō* in the third person singular:_____

	LATIN	ENGLISH
PRESENT ACT.		
FUTURE ACT.		
IMPERFECT ACT.		
PERFECT ACT.		

2. *mittō* in the third person plural: _____

	LATIN	ENGLISH
PRESENT ACT.		
FUTURE ACT.		
IMPERFECT ACT.		
PERFECT ACT.		

3. *clāmō* in the second person singular:_____

	LATIN	ENGLISH
PRESENT ACT.		
FUTURE ACT.		
IMPERFECT ACT.		
PERFECT ACT.		

H. Answer the questions about this week's quotation.

1. What does *lex tāliōnis* mean in English? _____

2. Give a phrase from the Bible that is an example of *lex tāliōnis:* _____

3. What is the case and number of *lex?* _____

4. *Tāliōnis* is the genitive singular of *tāliō.* Which declension is *tāliō* in? _____

I. Cross out the incorrect translation in each set.

1. gessī

    a) I have worn   b) I wore   c) I will wear

2. accēpērunt

    a) you all accepted   b) they did accept   c) they have accepted

3. sensistis

    a) you all felt   b) you all did feel   c) you all feel

4. cupīvimus

    a) we did want   b) we were wanting   c) we have wanted

5. surrēxit

    a) she does get up   b) she did get up   c) she did rise

J. Each sentence below uses a derivative (in italics). Use your knowledge of Latin to finish each sentence by circling the correct answer!

1. When someone sings *solo,* it means they are singing _____.

    a) far away   b) too loud   c) alone   d) well

2. A *message* is information you _____ to someone.

    a) sell   b) send   c) drive   d) show

3. *Legal* problems are problems connected to the _____.

    a) law   b) goal   c) mayor   d) neighborhood

K. Translate these sentences into English.

1. Proscrīptus equōs sumptuōsōs celeriter cēpit. _____

_____

2. Cupīvit equōs vendere et pecūniam accipere. _____

_____

3. Aedīlis fāmam audīvit, et īrātus erat. _____

_____

4. Armentāriī perītī clāmāvērunt, "Proscrīptum capiēmus et equōs conservābimus!" _____

_____

_____

5. Magnōs petasōs et vestēs pulvereās gessērunt. _____

_____

6. Armentāriī proscrīptum invēnērunt, sed sōlus nōn erat. _____

_____

7. Armentāriī et proscrīptī pugnant, et sclopēta ardent! _____

_____

8. Armentārius ferus clāmat, "Accipite fātum vel occidite!" _____

_____

9. Mox armentāriī proscrīptōs vīcērunt, et proscrīptī fūgērunt. _____

_____

10. Armentārius fessus et grātus dicit, "Sum famēlicus. Estisne?" _____

_____

Translate these sentences into Latin.

11. A hungry vulture watched the tired cow. _____

12. The large desert was dry and hot. _____

13. The cowboy rode a dark horse. _____

14. Did a lone wolf fight the dogs? _____

15. The frightened outlaw did not want to build a fire. _____

_____

[This page intentionally blank]

WEEK 22

Word List

NOUNS

1. carmen, carminis (n) . . . . . song, chant, poem
2. cervus, -ī (m) . . . . stag, deer
3. cor, cordis (n) . . . . heart
4. gaudium, gaudiī (n) . . . . . joy, happiness
5. mālum, -ī (n) . . . . apple
6. nānus, -ī (m) . . . . dwarf
7. nix, nivis (f) . . . . snow
8. osculum, -ī (n) . . . . kiss
9. rēgulus, -ī (m) . . . . prince
10. speculum, -ī (n) . . . . mirror
11. vēnātor, vēnātōris (m) . . . . hunter, huntsman
12. venēfica, -ae (f) . . . . witch

ADJECTIVES

13. niveus, -a, um . . . . snowy, snow white
14. venēnātus, -a, -um . . . . . . poisoned, enchanted

ADVERBS

15. iterum . . . . again, a second time

VERBS

16. cantō (1) . . . . I sing, play (an instrument)
17. urgeō, urgēre, ursī, ursum . . . . I urge
18. vocō (1) . . . . I call, summon, invite

Chant:

No new chant this week.

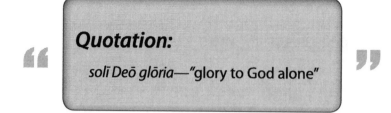

Weekly Worksheet 22

name:

A. Write the full names of the cases in order on these lines. Feel free to look below for a hint!

1. _____

2. _____

3. _____

4. _____

5. _____

B. Label each noun's declension (1, 2, 3, 3i, 4, or 5) and gender (M, F, or N). Then decline it.

DECLENSION _____ GENDER _____

	SINGULAR	PLURAL
NOM.	cor	
GEN.		
DAT.		
ACC.		
ABL.		

DECLENSION _____ GENDER _____

	SINGULAR	PLURAL
NOM.	rēgulus	
GEN.		
DAT.		
ACC.		
ABL.		

DECLENSION _____ GENDER _____

	SINGULAR	PLURAL
NOM.	venēfica	
GEN.		
DAT.		
ACC.		
ABL.		

DECLENSION _____ GENDER _____

	SINGULAR	PLURAL
NOM.	nix	
GEN.		
DAT.		
ACC.		
ABL.		

Now, go back through the nouns you've just declined and circle the dative case endings for each one.

C. Decline *enchanted apple*.

	SINGULAR	PLURAL
NOM.		
GEN.		
DAT.		
ACC.		
ABL.		

D. For each noun, list its gender and its singular and plural dative forms. Then translate the singular dative form into English.

	NOUN	GENDER	SINGULAR DATIVE	PLURAL DATIVE	TRANSLATION
1.	cervus				
2.	puella				
3.	mare				
4.	aedīlis				
5.	architectus				
6.	vēnātor				
7.	agricola				
8.	rēs				
9.	animal				
10.	vultur				
11.	nānus				
12.	māter				
13.	gaudium				

E. Fill in the blanks.

1. An indirect object tells you *to* _____ or *for* _____ the verb is done.

2. In Latin, which case do you use for the indirect object? _____

3. Which two English words do you often use to translate Latin indirect objects? _____

4. Which case do you use for the subject? _____

5. Which case do you use for the direct object? _____

6. An adjective must always match the _____, _____, and

_____ of the noun it modifies.

F. For each noun, give its case—nominative (N), accusative (A), or dative (D)—and number (S or P). If there is more than one possibility, list them all. (Do not list cases besides these.) The first one is done for you.

1. nivī _____ DS _____   5. carminibus_____   9. rēgulīs_____

2. gaudiō _____   6. armentārium _____   10. mēlī _____

3. cor _____   7. hērōī_____   11. proscrīptō _____

4. speculīs _____   8. incolae_____   12. patribus _____

G. In each English sentence, underline the direct object and circle the indirect object. Translate the indirect object into Latin and write it the blank. (Remember which case the indirect object takes!) An example is given below.

I threw <u>the baseball</u> to (a friend)   __amīcō__

1. The girl gave flowers to her mother. _____

2. The people had a gift for the brave cowboy. _____

3. My dog brought me the stick. _____

4. Can I cut a piece of cake for you? _____

5. The lieutenant sent a long answer to the general. _____

6. I offered crackers to the parrots. _____

7. May I bring you all anything else? _____

8. The king had a message for the witch. _____

H. Translate this story into English. The story includes a few indirect objects, which will be in the dative case. In the Latin, underline all direct objects and circle all indirect objects.

Virgō avibus et cervīs carmina cantāvit. Mātrem vel patrem nōn habuit. Mulier erat alba, et capillōs nigrōs et ōs rubrum habuit. Virgō erat Nivea. Multīs nānīs cibum fēcit, et erant amīcī bonī. Sed venēfica mala virginem pulchram nōn amāvit. Venēfica Niveae mālum venēnātum dedit. Nivea occidit, sed rēgulus mīrus Niveam invēnit. Dedit Niveae osculum. Vītam iterum habuit!

_____

_____

_____

_____

_____

_____

_____

_____

I. Translate these English sentences into Latin. When you finish, circle any Latin words in the dative.

1. The wicked queen gave the huntsman a horrible hardship. _____

_____

2. The cunning huntsman will give a heart to the queen. _____

_____

3. The witch spoke to the magical mirror. _____

4. The impartial mirror tells the witch a strange poem._____

_____

5. The prince wants to find Snow White quickly. _____

J. Answer the following questions about this week's quotation.

1. How do you say "glory to God alone" in Latin? _____

2. Which famous composer often wrote an abbreviation of this phrase on his music? _____

3. List the case and number of each word:_____

_____

K. Give a synopsis for each of the following verbs.

1. *vocō* in the first person singular:_____

	LATIN	ENGLISH
PRESENT ACT.		
FUTURE ACT.		
IMPERFECT ACT.		
PERFECT ACT.		

2. *cantō* in the third person singular: _____

	LATIN	ENGLISH
PRESENT ACT.		
FUTURE ACT.		
IMPERFECT ACT.		
PERFECT ACT.		

3. *urgeō* in the second person plural: _____

	LATIN	ENGLISH
PRESENT ACT.		
FUTURE ACT.		
IMPERFECT ACT.		
PERFECT ACT.		

WEEK 23

Word List

NOUNS

1. ager, agrī (m) . . . . field
2. exemplum, -ī (n) . . . . example, sample
3. fax, facis (f) . . . . torch, firebrand
4. fūnis, fūnis (m) . . . . rope
5. homō, hominis (m) . . . . . person, man, human being
6. iuvenis, iuvenis (m/f) . . . . young person, young man, young woman
7. marmor, marmoris (n). . . . . marble
8. onus, oneris (n). . . . . burden, load, weight
9. saepēs, saepis (f) . . . . hedge, fence
10. secūris, secūris (f). . . . . . axe, hatchet
11. senex, senis (m) . . . . old man
12. tyrannus, -ī (m) . . . . tyrant

ADJECTIVES

13. ponderōsus, -a, -um . . . . . heavy

ADVERBS

14. semper . . . . always

VERBS

15. circumdō, circumdāre, circumdedī, circumdatum . . I put *something* (acc.) around *something* (dat.)
16. dēclārō (1) . . . . I declare, make clear
17. mandō (1). . . . . I entrust, command
18. postulō (1) . . . . I demand

Chant:

No new chant this week.

Quotation:

Sīc semper tyrannīs—"Thus always to tyrants"

Weekly Worksheet 23

name:

A. Fill in the blanks.

1. Which part of speech tells you *to whom* or *for whom* the verb is done? _____

2. Which case do you use for this part of speech? _____

3. Which two English words do you often use to translate Latin indirect objects? _____

4. Which case do you use for the direct object? _____

5. Which case do you use for predicate nouns? _____

6. An adjective must always match the noun it modifies in _____, _____,

and _____.

B. Label each noun's declension (1, 2, 3, 3i, 4, or 5) and gender (M, F, or N). Then decline it. Circle the dative endings.

DECLENSION _____ GENDER _____

	SINGULAR	PLURAL
NOM.	exemplum	
GEN.		
DAT.		
ACC.		
ABL.		

DECLENSION _____ GENDER _____

	SINGULAR	PLURAL
	saepēs	

C. For each noun, give its nominative, genitive, and dative singular forms.

	NOUN	NOMINATIVE	GENITIVE	DATIVE
1.	old man			
2.	young person			

	NOUN	NOMINATIVE	GENITIVE	DATIVE
3.	tyrant			
4.	field			
5.	torch			
6.	hedge			
7.	marble			
8.	person			
9.	rope			
10.	queen			
11.	axe			
12.	army			
13.	burden			
14.	master			
15.	ox			

D. Using at least two of the nouns above, write a Latin sentence. One noun in the sentence must be in the dative case. Give the translation of your sentence.

_____

_____

_____

_____

E. Decline *heavy statue*.

	SINGULAR	PLURAL
NOM.		
GEN.		
DAT.		
ACC.		
ABL.		

F. In each English sentence, underline the direct object and circle the indirect object. Translate the indirect object into Latin and write it the blank. (Remember which case the indirect object takes!)

1. The old man gave us his opinion. _____

2. The prince will never swear loyalty to the tyrant! _____

3. Austin gave his compliments to the chef. _____

4. I found a place for the load. _____

5. Dad bought some shears for the hedges. _____

G. For each Latin sentence, write the case (Nom., Dat., Acc.) above the nouns and the tense (Pres., Fut., Imp., Perf.) and person (1, 2, 3) above the verbs. Then translate the sentence.

1. Senex lucum hospitibus dēmonstrāvit. _____

_____

2. Mulier adulēscēntī exemplum dabat. _____

_____

3. Senī onus portābis. _____

4. Puella donum amicō grātō mīsit. _____

5. Pater fabulās līberīs quiētīs recitābat. _____

_____

6. Architectō marmor ponderōsum et nigrum semper dabimus! _____

_____

7. Tyrannus sententiam populō hodiē dēclārābit. _____

_____

8. Homō celeriter currit et custōdī facem dat. _____

_____

Translate these English sentences into Latin. When you finish, circle any Latin words in the dative.

9. The tyrant gives gold to the gangster. _____

10. The farmer showed the hedgehogs to the children. _____

_____

11. The hunter entrusted an axe to the young person. _____

_____

12. The angry citizens demand to see the tyrant. _____

_____

H. Practice using *circumdō* by translating these sentences. Remember, *circumdō* means "to put something (acc.) around something (dat.)."

1. Vestem iuvenī circumdat. _____

2. Bracchium matrī circumdedit. _____

3. Exercitūs oppidō circumdedērunt. _____

4. Armentāriī saepem agrō circumdābant. _____

_____

5. Senex fūnem canī circumdedit. _____

I. Answer the following questions about this week's quotation.

1. How do you say "Thus always to tyrants" in Latin? _____

2. Which state has this as their motto? _____

3. Which word means "tyrants"? _____

4. What is its gender, number, and case? _____

J. Here are some derivatives from this week's Word List. Look up each word's definition (online or in a dictionary) and write it on the lines. In the parentheses, write each word's Latin root.

1. marmoreal: _____ (_____)

2. funambulist: _____ (_____)

3. agriculture: _____

_____ (_____)

K. Give a synopsis for each of the following verbs.

1. *dēclārō* in the first person plural: _____

	LATIN	ENGLISH
PRESENT ACT.		
FUTURE ACT.		
IMPERFECT ACT.		
PERFECT ACT.		

2. *mandō* in the second person singular: _____

	LATIN	ENGLISH
PRESENT ACT.		
FUTURE ACT.		
IMPERFECT ACT.		
PERFECT ACT.		

3. *postulō* in the third person plural: _____

	LATIN	ENGLISH
PRESENT ACT.		
FUTURE ACT.		
IMPERFECT ACT.		
PERFECT ACT.		

L. On the lines below, give the Latin word for each picture.

1. _____   2. _____   3. _____   4. _____

5. _____   6. _____   7. _____   8. _____

WEEK 24

Word List

NOUNS

1. elephantus, -ī (m/f) . . . . . . elephant

2. mūs, mūris (m/f) . . . . mouse, rat

ADJECTIVES

3. stultus, -a, -um . . . . foolish, silly

VERBS

4. placeō, placēre, placuī, placitum (with dat.) . . I please, am acceptable to

5. vexō (1) . . . . I shake, toss, harrass, annoy

Chant:

No new chant this week.

Quotation:

No new quotation this week.

Weekly Worksheet 24

name: _____

A. Fill in the blanks.

1. List the principal parts of *aperiō:* _____

2. Which conjugation is *aperiō* in? _____

3. Which family is it in? _____

4. How do you find the present stem of *aperiō?* _____

5. What is the present stem of *aperiō?* _____

6. List the principal parts of *iaciō:* _____

7. Which conjugation is *iaciō* in? _____

8. Is it a third conjugation *-iō* verb or not? _____

9. How do you know? _____

_____

10. Do third conjugation *-iō* verbs conjugate more like the third conjugation or the fourth

conjugation? _____

11. The word that *receives the action of the verb* is called the _____ .

12. Which Latin case do you use for this type of word? _____

13. The word that tells you _____ *whom* or _____ *whom* the verb is done is

the indirect object.

14. Which case do you use for this type of word? _____

15. *Circumdō* means "I put *something* (in the _____ case) around *something* (in

the _____ case)."

B. In the boxes below, write the endings for the perfect tense. Then answer the questions.

	SINGULAR	PLURAL
1ST		
2ND		
3RD		

1. Which tense are these endings for? _____

2. Which stem do these endings attach to? _____

3. How do you find the perfect stem of a verb? _____

_____

4. Is this how you find the perfect stem for *every* conjugation? _____

C. Label each noun's declension (1, 2, 3, 3i, 4, or 5) and gender (M, F, or N). Then decline it. Circle the dative endings.

DECLENSION _____ GENDER _____

	SINGULAR	PLURAL
NOM.	elephantus	
GEN.		
DAT.		
ACC.		
ABL.		

DECLENSION _____ GENDER _____

	SINGULAR	PLURAL
NOM.	mūs	
GEN.		
DAT.		
ACC.		
ABL.		

D. For each noun, give its gender and its singular and plural dative forms. Then translate the singular dative form into English.

	NOUN	GENDER	SINGULAR DATIVE	PLURAL DATIVE	TRANSLATION
1.	aedīlis				
2.	victor				

	NOUN	GENDER	SINGULAR DATIVE	PLURAL DATIVE	TRANSLATION
3.	rēgulus				
4.	māter				
5.	amīcus				
6.	agricola				
7.	tyrannus				
8.	venēfica				

E. Decline *lone tree.* (Remember, *sōlus* declines unusually in the genitive and dative singular!)

	SINGULAR	PLURAL
NOM.		
GEN.		
DAT.		
ACC.		
ABL.		

F. Fill in the principal parts. In the parentheses at the end of the line, write which conjugation each verb is in (1, 2, 3, 3io, or 4).

1. vexō, _____, _____, _____ (_____)

2. urgeō, _____, _____, _____ (_____)

3. iaciō, _____, _____, _____ (_____)

4. circumdō, _____, _____, _____ (_____)

5. gerō, _____, _____, _____ (_____)

6. doceō, _____, _____, _____ (_____)

7. iaciō, _____, _____, _____ (_____)

8. sciō, _____, _____, _____ (_____)

9. vocō, _____, _____, _____ (_____)

10. fugiō, _____, _____, _____ (_____)

11. scandō, _____, _____, _____ (_____)

12. saliō, _____, _____, _____ (_____)

13. cupiō, _____, _____, _____ (_____)

14. surgō, _____, _____, _____ (_____)

15. tussiō, _____, _____, _____ (_____)

G. Translate the Latin words into English, and the English words into Latin.

1. imber _____

2. mirror _____

3. vestis _____

4. benevolentia _____

5. auris _____

6. you climb _____

7. fātum _____

8. iūs _____

9. exemplum _____

10. tardē _____

11. or _____

12. stultum _____

13. we will sing _____

14. hat _____

15. ēricius _____

16. they built _____

17. goal _____

18. ponderōsa _____

19. semper _____

20. vastitās _____

21. scopulus _____

22. I felt _____

23. funny _____

24. never _____

25. ovis _____

26. marmor _____

27. holus _____

28. -que _____

29. iterum _____

30. vulpēs _____

H. Give a synopsis for each of the following verbs.

1. *lūdō* in the third person singular: _____

	LATIN	ENGLISH
PRESENT ACT.		
FUTURE ACT.		
IMPERFECT ACT.		
PERFECT ACT.		

2. *accipiō* in the second person plural: _____

	LATIN	ENGLISH
PRESENT ACT.		
FUTURE ACT.		
IMPERFECT ACT.		
PERFECT ACT.		

3. *audiō* in the first person plural: _____

	LATIN	ENGLISH
PRESENT ACT.		
FUTURE ACT.		
IMPERFECT ACT.		
PERFECT ACT.		

4. *placeō* in the second person singular: _____

	LATIN	ENGLISH
PRESENT ACT.		
FUTURE ACT.		
IMPERFECT ACT.		
PERFECT ACT.		

I. Complete the Latin quotations, and give the English meaning of each.

1. Tempus _____ : _____

2. _____ Deō glōria: _____

3. Senātus _____ Rōmānus: _____

4. Sīc _____ _____ : _____

5. Vēnī, _____ , _____ : _____

J. Translate these sentences into English.

1. Mūs pulvereus et famēlicus semper elephantum vexāvit. _____

_____

2. Cursūs longī sciūrīs citīs semper placent. _____

_____

3. Mūs elephantō parvō pinnam nigram dat. _____

_____

4. Saepēs āridae et brūnae rēgīnae nōn placuērunt. _____

_____

5. Victor exercitibus misericordiam dēmonstrāvit._____

_____

6. Aedīlēs populō lēgēs recitāre parābant._____

_____

7. Testūdō ēriciīs iūs calidum facit. _____

_____

8. Dominus elephantīs callidīs nucleōs iterum dedit. _____

_____

9. Dabisne mihi vestem novam rubram? _____

10. Tyrannus fūnēs circumdābat effigiēī pulchrae. _____

_____

Translate these English sentences into Latin.

11. The happy guest is singing funny songs for the children. _____

_____

12. You never want to fight a badger and a wolf at the same time. _____

_____

13. The hungry outlaws gave much praise to the chef. _____

_____

14. The rumor is silly and amusing, but it annoys the old man._____

_____

15. Feel (sg.) the cold, heavy marble. _____

K. Match each English derivative with its Latin root. On the lines, give the meaning of each Latin word.

1. vermicelli

mittō _____

2. vestige

osculum _____

3. chant

pulcher _____

4. missile

vermis _____

5. elephantine

fugiō _____

6. osculate

cantō _____

7. fugitive

mūs _____

8. muscle

vestīgium _____

9. onerous

elephantus _____

10. pulchritudinous

onus _____

L. On the lines below, give the Latin word for each picture.

1. _____   2. _____   3. _____   4. _____

4 UNIT FOUR

UNIT 4: GOALS

Weeks 25–32

By the end of Unit 4, students should be able to . . .

- Recognize, form, and translate prepositions with accusative objects
- Recognize, form, and translate prepositions with ablative objects
- Recognize, form, and translate the ablative of time
- Give the principal parts for any verb from the Word Lists

WEEK 25

Word List

NOUNS

1. castellum, -ī (n) . . . . castle
2. cōpia, -ae (f). . . . . supply
   plural: cōpiae, -ārum. . . . . troops, supplies
3. famēs, famis (f) . . . . famine, hunger, starvation
4. lacus, lacūs (m) . . . . lake, tub, hollow
5. legiō, legiōnis (f) . . . . legion
6. līmen, līminis (n) . . . . doorway, threshold
7. mīles, mīlitis (m/f) . . . . . . soldier
8. tectum, -ī (n) . . . . roof, building, dwelling
9. turris, turris (f). . . . . tower, turret
10. urbs, urbis (f) . . . . city
11. vallēs, vallis (f) . . . . valley
12. virtūs, virtūtis (f) . . . . . . manliness, courage, strength

VERBS

13. accūsō (1). . . . . I accuse, blame
14. secō, secāre, secuī, sectum. . . . . I cut
15. stō, stāre, stetī, statum. . . . . I stand

PREPOSITIONS

16. in (with acc.) . . . . into
17. per (with acc.) . . . . through
18. trans (with acc.) . . . . across

Chant:

No new chant this week.

Quotation:

in mediās rēs—"into the middle of things"

Weekly Worksheet 25

name:

A. Fill in the blanks.

1. A preposition connects a _____ or pronoun to the rest of a sentence.

2. That noun or pronoun is called the _____ of the preposition.

3. *Prepositional phrase* is another name for a _____ and its _____

(and any modifiers).

4. The preposition *trans* always takes a noun in the _____ case.

5. The preposition *per* always takes a noun in the _____ case.

6. The preposition *in* means "_____" when paired with a noun in the

_____ case.

B. Translate these prepositional phrases into English. Underline the object of each Latin preposition.

1. per limen _____

2. in urbem _____

3. trans viam _____

4. in lacum _____

5. per vallem _____

6. per fenestrās _____

7. trans agrōs _____

8. per vastitātēs _____

9. in imbrem _____

10. in perīcula _____

C. Translate these prepositional phrases into Latin. Underline the object of each English preposition.

1. across the valley _____

2. through the cities _____

3. into a tower _____

4. through a story _____

5. into the fire _____

6. into wine _____

7. through the mirror _____

8. across stones _____

9. through the days _____

10. across time _____

D. These prepositional phrases include adjectives. Translate them into English.

1. trans maria gelida _____

2. per oppidum pulvereum _____

3. into a horrible famine _____

4. in turrēs albās _____

5. trans cavum magnum _____

6. per saepem densam _____

7. in prōvinciam novam _____

8. per indicem callidum _____

E. These sentences all use prepositional phrases. Underline the preposition and its object (and any adjective modifying the object), and translate the sentences into English.

1. Mīlitēs trans vallem clāmant. _____

2. Fulmen per mōntēs sonāvit. _____

_____

3. Fēlēs nigra trans tectum ambulābat. _____

_____

4. Pater per pānem calidum secuit. _____

5. Pīrātae per gurgitēs mox nāvigābunt. _____

_____

6. Ovēs ferae trans scopulōs celsōs scandunt. _____

_____

7. Venēfica in rēgīnam pulchram mūtāvit. _____

_____

8. Proscrīptus per fenestram novam saluit. _____

_____

Translate these sentences into Latin. Underline all the English prepositions.

9. The hero rides through the quiet town. _____

10. The heavy axe cut into the tree. _____

11. The princes ran through the large castle. _____

_____

12. We will walk across the city tomorrow. _____

F. For each noun, give its genitive singular form, gender (M, F, or N), base, and translation.

	NOUN	GENITIVE	GENDER	BASE	TRANSLATION
1.	castellum				
2.	famēs				
3.	virtūs				
4.	urbs				
5.	cōpia				
6.	līmen				
7.	turris				
8.	vallēs				
9.	legiō				
10.	mīles				
11.	lacus				
12.	tectum				
13.	cinis				
14.	gelū				

G. Answer the following questions about this week's quotation.

  1. How do you say "into the middle of things" in Latin?_____

  2. Which word is the preposition? _____

  3. What is the object of the preposition? _____

  4. What is the gender, number, and case of the object? _____

  5. What is the gender, number, and case of the adjective? _____

H. Here are two derivatives from this week's Word List. Look up each word's definition (online or in a dictionary) and write it on the lines. In the parentheses, write each word's Latin root.

  1. bisect: _____ (_____)

  2. chateau:_____

  _____ (_____)

I. Give a synopsis for each of the following verbs.

  1. *stō* in the third person singular: _____

	LATIN	ENGLISH
PRESENT ACT.		
FUTURE ACT.		
IMPERFECT ACT.		
PERFECT ACT.		

  2. *secō* in the first person plural:_____

	LATIN	ENGLISH
PRESENT ACT.		
FUTURE ACT.		
IMPERFECT ACT.		
PERFECT ACT.		

3. *accūsō* in the second person singular: _____

	LATIN	ENGLISH
PRESENT ACT.		
FUTURE ACT.		
IMPERFECT ACT.		
PERFECT ACT.		

J. You know three questions which identify whether a third declension noun is an i-stem. Fill in the blanks to complete the questions.

1. Does the noun's nominative singular end in _____ or _____ *and* have the same

number of _____ in the nominative and _____ singular? If so, then it is an

i-stem.

2. Does the noun's nominative singular end in _____or _____*and* have a base ending in

two _____? If so, then it is an i-stem.

3. Does the neuter noun's nominative singular end in _____, _____, or _____? If so,

then it is a _____ i-stem.

K. Now, using the i-stem questions, tell whether each of the following nouns is an i-stem (Yes or No), and if it is, which question tells you (1, 2, or 3).

1. vallēs, vallis _____   6. urbs, urbis _____

2. legiō, legiōnis _____   7. lacus, lacūs _____

3. līmen, līminis _____   8. famēs, famis _____

4. turris, turris _____   9. mīles, mīlitis _____

5. virtūs, virtūtis_____   10. saepēs, saepis _____

[This page intentionally blank]

WEEK 26

Word List

NOUNS

1. angustiae, -ārum (f, pl.) . . . . . . narrows, narrow pass, difficulties

2. aquila, -ae (f) . . . . eagle

3. caelum, -ī (n) . . . . sky, heaven

4. culmen, culminis (n) . . . . top, peak, high point

5. gladius, -ī (m) . . . . sword

6. latebra, -ae (f) . . . . hiding place, hideout, lair

7. nuntius, -ī (m) . . . . messenger

8. palūs, palūdis (f) . . . . swamp, bog

9. sagitta, -ae (f) . . . . arrow

10. scūtum, -ī (n) . . . . shield

11. tenebrae, tenebrārum (f, pl.) . . darkness, gloomy place, shadows

12. vallum, -ī (n) . . . . rampart, wall

ADJECTIVES

13. arduus, -a, -um . . . . steep, lofty

VERBS

14. nuntiō (1) . . . . I announce

15. veniō, venīre, vēnī, ventum . . . I come

16. volō (1) . . . . I fly

PREPOSITIONS

17. ad (with acc.) . . . . to, toward

18. ante (with acc.) . . . . before

19. post (with acc.) . . . . after, behind

Chant:

No new chant this week.

> **Quotation:**
>
> *ante merīdiem* (a.m.)—"before noon"
>
> *post merīdiem* (p.m.)—"after noon"

Weekly Worksheet 26

name:

A. For each noun, give its genitive singular form, gender (M, F, or N), base, and translation.

	NOUN	GENITIVE	GENDER	BASE	TRANSLATION
1.	scūtum				
2.	latebra				
3.	culmen				
4.	aquila				
5.	gladius				
6.	auris				
7.	merīdiēs				
8.	palūs				
9.	mūs				
10.	vallum				
11.	sagitta				
12.	gradus				

B. Each of these nouns exists only in the plural. For each one, give its genitive plural form, gender (M, F, or N), base, and translation.

	NOUN	GENITIVE	GENDER	BASE	TRANSLATION
1.	tenebrae				
2.	līberī				
3.	angustiae				

C. Give a synopsis for each of the following verbs.

1. *nuntiō* in the second person plural: _____

	LATIN	ENGLISH
PRESENT ACT.		
FUTURE ACT.		
IMPERFECT ACT.		
PERFECT ACT.		

2. *volō* in the third person singular: _____

	LATIN	ENGLISH
PRESENT ACT.		
FUTURE ACT.		
IMPERFECT ACT.		
PERFECT ACT.		

3. *veniō* in the first person singular: _____

	LATIN	ENGLISH
PRESENT ACT.		
FUTURE ACT.		
IMPERFECT ACT.		
PERFECT ACT.		

D. Fill in the blanks.

1. A _____ connects a noun or pronoun to the rest of a sentence.

2. That noun or pronoun is called the _____ of the _____.

3. *Prepositional phrase* is another name for a _____ and its _____

(and any modifiers).

4. The preposition *ad* always takes a noun in the _____ case.

5. The preposition *ante* always takes a noun in the _____ case.

6. The preposition *post* always takes a noun in the _____ case.

E. Translate these prepositional phrases into English.

1. ad palūdem _____

2. post tenebrās _____

3. per angustiās _____

4. trans vallum _____

5. in latebram _____

6. ante tempestātem _____

7. ad culmen _____

8. post famēs _____

9. ad virtūtem _____

10. ante speculum _____

F. Translate these prepositional phrases into Latin.

1. behind the wheel _____

2. into the shield _____

3. after the rain _____

4. toward the castles _____

5. across the bog _____

6. into songs _____

7. before the hedges _____

8. to difficulties _____

9. before me _____

10. after dinner _____

G. These prepositional phrases include adjectives. Translate them into English.

1. in palūdēs horrendās _____

2. trans culmina ardua _____

3. ad latebram niveam _____

4. post prīmum elephantum _____

5. ante līmen pulvereum_____

H. These sentences all use prepositional phrases. Underline each prepositional phrase (including adjectives modifying the object of the preposition), and translate the sentences into English.

1. Scūtum magicum post vallum invēnimus. _____

_____

2. Gladius clārus per tenebrās secuit. _____

_____

3. Famula ad populum vocāvit, "Venite ante rēgem!" _____

_____

4. Mīlitēs multās sagittās ad valla mīsērunt._____

_____

5. Mercātor cāseum novum trans oppidum invenit. _____

_____

6. Aquila per caelum ad culmen arduum volāvit. _____

_____

7. Multa animālia post nōs ambulāvērunt, et equus albus ante nōs volāvit._____

_____

8. Carrus adulēscēntem per urbem ad medicum portāvit. _____

_____

9. Latrōnēs pecuniam cēpērunt et ad latebram currunt!_____

_____

10. Nuntius citus litterās trans regiōnem herī portāvit. _____

_____

Translate these sentences into Latin.

11. I am not able to clean the bog for you. _____

12. The master put watchmen around the ramparts. _____

_____

13. The fleet came to the narrows before us. _____

_____

14. Are you flying to the distant island soon? _____

_____

15. After the fire, the people wanted to build a new city. _____

_____

I. Answer the following questions about this week's quotation.

1. How do you say "before noon" in Latin? _____

2. How do we normally abbreviate this phrase? _____

3. Which case is the object of the preposition in? _____

4. How do you say "after noon" in Latin? _____

5. How do we normally abbreviate this phrase? _____

6. What is the gender, number, and case of the noun? _____

J. Match each English derivative with its Latin root. On the lines, give the meaning of each Latin word.

1. wall   gladius _____

2. gladiola   aquila _____

3. arduous   arduus _____

4. tenebrous   vallum _____

5. aquiline   tenebrae _____

K. Give the masculine, feminine, and neuter dative singular of these adjectives in Latin.

	ADJECTIVE	MASCULINE	FEMININE	NEUTER
1.	steep			
2.	enchanted			
3.	heavy			
4.	only			

WEEK 27

Word List

NOUNS

1. ariēna, -ae (f) . . . . .banana
2. camēlopardalis, camēlopardalis (f). . . . .giraffe
3. caput, capitis (n) . . . . .head
4. cauda, -ae (f) . . . . .tail
5. crocodīlus, -ī (m) . . . . .crocodile
6. hippopotamus, -ī (m) . . . . .hippopotamus, hippo
7. manus, -ūs (f) . . . . .hand
8. mēlo, mēlōnis (m) . . . . .melon
9. nāsus, -ī (m) . . . . .nose
10. oculus, -ī (m). . . . . .eye
11. sīmia, -ae (f) . . . . .ape, monkey
12. strūthiocamēlus, -ī (m) . . . . .ostrich

ADJECTIVES

13. dūrus, -a, -um . . . . .hard, tough, difficult
14. rotundus, -a, -um. . . . . .round, circular

VERBS

15. appropinquō (1) (with *ad* + acc.) . . . .I approach, draw near
16. pōnō, pōnere, posuī, positum . . . . .I put, place
17. pulsō (1). . . . . .I strike, beat
18. tollō, tollere, sustulī, sublātum. . . . . .I pick up, lift, raise
19. trahō, trahere, traxī, tractum . . . . . . .I pull, draw, drag

PREPOSITIONS

20. propter (with acc.) . . . . .on account of, because of

Chant:

No new chant this week.

Quotation:

post hoc ergō propter hoc—"after this, therefore because of this"

Weekly Worksheet 27 *name:*

A. For each noun, give its base, gender (M, F, or N), declension (1, 2, 3, 3i, 4, or 5), and translation.

	NOUN	BASE	GENDER	DECLENSION	TRANSLATION
1.	sīmia				
2.	caput				
3.	onus				
4.	cor				
5.	camēlopardalis				
6.	mēlo				
7.	oculus				
8.	angustiae				
9.	manus				
10.	cauda				
11.	faciēs				
12.	nāsus				
13.	ariēna				
14.	urbs				
15.	hippopotamus				

B. Underline the adjective that goes with the noun (watch the case!) and then translate the phrase.

NOUN   ADJECTIVE   TRANSLATION

1. sīmiam   famēlica / famēlicam / famēlicae   _____

2. crocodīlīs   callidī / callidōs / callidīs   _____

NOUN	ADJECTIVE	TRANSLATION
3. ariēna	dūra / dūrum / dūram	_____
4. mēlōnēs	flāvō / flāvīs / flāvōs	_____
5. hippopotamus	rotundus / rotunda / rotundōs	_____

C. Decline *tough ostrich*.

	SINGULAR	PLURAL
NOM.		
GEN.		
DAT.		
ACC.		
ABL.		

D. Fill in the principal parts for each of the following verbs, and circle the perfect stem. In the parentheses at the end of the line, write which conjugation each verb is in (1, 2, 3, 3io, 4, or IRR [irregular]).

1. trahō, _____, _____, _____ (_____)

2. veniō, _____, _____, _____ (_____)

3. secō, _____, _____, _____ (_____)

4. placeō, _____, _____, _____ (_____)

5. occidō, _____, _____, _____ (_____)

6. circumdō, _____, _____, _____ (_____)

7. possum, _____, _____, _____ (_____)

8. postulō, _____, _____, _____ (_____)

9. pulsō, _____, _____, _____ (_____)

10. accipiō, _____, _____, _____ (_____)

C. Give a synopsis for each of the following verbs.

1. *tollō* in the third person plural: _____

	LATIN	ENGLISH
PRESENT ACT.		
FUTURE ACT.		
IMPERFECT ACT.		
PERFECT ACT.		

2. *appropinquō* in the second person singular: _____

_____

	LATIN	ENGLISH
PRESENT ACT.		
FUTURE ACT.		
IMPERFECT ACT.		
PERFECT ACT.		

3. *pōnō* in the first person plural: _____

	LATIN	ENGLISH
PRESENT ACT.		
FUTURE ACT.		
IMPERFECT ACT.		
PERFECT ACT.		

D. Fill in the blanks.

1. A preposition connects a _____ or pronoun to the rest of a _____.

2. That noun or pronoun is called the _____ of the preposition.

3. *Prepositional phrase* is another name for a _____ and its _____ (and

any modifiers).

4. The preposition *propter* always takes an object in the _____ case.

E. Practice using *appropinquō* by translating these sentences. Remember, to say what is being approached, you use *appropinquō* combined with *ad* + an accusative object. An example is given below.

Ad strūthiocamēlum appropinquābam.   *I was approaching the ostrich.*

1. Ad hippopotamum quiētum appropinquāvimus. _____

_____

2. Camēlopardalēs ad arborēs celsās appropinquābant._____

_____

3. Classēs ad pīrātās celeriter appropinquant. _____

_____

4. Appropinquābitne sīmia ad nōs? _____

5. Nuntius fessus appropinquāvit ad harēnam. _____

_____

F. Translate these prepositional phrases into English.

1. propter testimōnium_____

2. post strūthiocamēlōs _____

3. propter sīmiam parvam _____

4. in mēlōnem āridum _____

5. propter multa exempla bona _____

G. Translate these prepositional phrases into Latin.

1. on account of a horse _____

2. because of the difficult mountains_____

3. through new eyes _____

4. because of the harsh tyrant _____

5. across the distant athletic field _____

H. Translate these sentences into English. Underline any prepositional phrases.

1. Sīmiae propter ariēnam sōlam pugnābant. _____

_____

2. Camēlopardalis leōnem calcitrāvit, sed leō appropinquāre pergit!_____

_____

3. Strūthiocamēlus in hārenam caput pōnit. _____

_____

4. Possumusne hippopotamum ponderōsum trahere per aquam? _____

_____

5. Crocodīlus callidus rīsit et multōs dentēs albōs dēmonstrāvit. _____

_____

6. Aedīlis aurum et argentum propter latrōnēs occultat._____

_____

7. Mēlōnem dūrum pulsō, sed nōn aperiet! _____

_____

8. Amīcī in lacum propter diem calidum saluērunt. _____

_____

9. Strūthiocamēlus, sīmia, et camēlopardalis elephantum cūriōsum parvum propter fāmam

pulsāvērunt. _____

_____

10. Nunc elephantus parvus nāsum longum habet et multās rēs tollere potest. _____

_____

Translate these sentences into Latin.

11. Put (sg.) the melons and bananas into the cart. _____

_____

12. Will you give me a hand? _____

13. The man is tired because of the hard day. _____

_____

14. The king approached the trembling informer. _____

_____

15. I was pulling a red cart behind you all. _____

I. Answer the following questions about this week's quotation.

1. What does *post hoc ergō propter hoc* mean? _____

2. What part of speech is *post?* _____

3. What part of speech is *propter?* _____

4. What case do their objects always take? _____

J. On the lines below, give the Latin word for each picture.

1. _____ 2. _____ 3. _____ 4. _____

5. _____ 6. _____ 7. _____ 8. _____

[This page intentionally blank]

WEEK 28

Word List

NOUNS

1. arca, -ae (f). . . . . box, chest

2. arcanum, -ī (n) . . . . secret

3. captīvus, -ī (m) . . . . captive, prisoner

4. crepida, -ae (f) . . . . slipper, sandal

5. dīvitiae, -ārum (f, pl.). . . . . riches, wealth

6. familia, -ae (f) . . . . household, family

7. forum, -ī (n) . . . . public square, marketplace

8. lōdix, lōdīcis (f) . . . . blanket, rug

9. placenta, -ae (f). . . . . cake

10. pulvis, pulveris (m) . . . . . . dust, powder

ADJECTIVES

11. generōsus, -a, -um . . . . . . generous, noble

12. suspīciōsus, -a, -um . . . . . suspicious

VERBS

13. dēcipiō, dēcipere, dēcēpī, dēceptum . . . I trick, deceive

14. hiemō (1) . . . . I spend the winter

15. hilarō (1) . . . . I cheer up, gladden

16. teneō, tenēre, tenuī, tentum . . . . I hold, keep

PREPOSITIONS

17. cum (with abl.). . . . . with

18. in (with abl.) . . . . in, on

Chant:

No new chant this week.

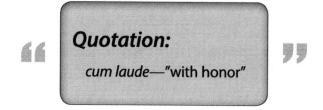

Quotation:

cum laude—"with honor"

Weekly Worksheet 28   *name:*

A. Label each noun's declension (1, 2, 3, 3i, 4, or 5) and gender (M, F, or N), then decline it. Circle the ablative endings.

DECLENSION _____   GENDER _____

	SINGULAR	PLURAL
NOM.	captīvus	
GEN.		
DAT.		
ACC.		
ABL.		

DECLENSION _____   GENDER _____

	SINGULAR	PLURAL
NOM.	placenta	
GEN.		
DAT.		
ACC.		
ABL.		

B. For each noun, give its base and its singular and plural ablative forms.

	NOUN	BASE	SINGULAR ABLATIVE	PLURAL ABLATIVE
1.	dust			
2.	secret			
3.	marketplace			
4.	wealth		————	
5.	rug			
6.	hope			
7.	slipper			
8.	household			
9.	box			
10.	army			

C. Cross out any nouns *not* in the ablative case.

nāsīs	crocodīlō	ariēna	angustiīs	scūtō	rētī
urbe	legiōnēs	līminī	mūre	līmīs	sclopētōs
mīlitibus	mēlōne	hospitis	effigiē	iūre	glaciēbus
rēgīnā	fenestrīs	maribus	lacuī	vīsū	mercātōre

D. Give the singular and plural ablative endings for each declension.

	DECLENSION	SINGULAR ABLATIVE	PLURAL ABLATIVE
1.	first		
2.	second		
3.	second neuter		
4.	third		
5.	third neuter		
6.	third i-stem		
7.	third i-stem neuter		
8.	fourth		
9.	fourth neuter		
10.	fifth		

E. Fill in the blanks.

1. A preposition _____ a noun or pronoun to the rest of a sentence.

2. That noun or pronoun is called the _____ of the preposition.

3. *Prepositional phrase* is another name for a preposition and its _____ (and any modifiers).

4. The preposition *cum* always takes a noun in the _____ case.

5. In a prepositional phrase with an adjective, *cum* likes to go _____ the object and the

adjective.

6. When *cum* is paired with a first or second person pronoun (*mē, tē, nōbis, vōbis*), it attaches to the

_____ of the pronoun.

7. Write "with us" in Latin: _____

8. The preposition *in* means "in, on" when paired with a noun in the _____ case.

F. Translate these prepositional phrases into English. Underline the ending of the object.

1. cum captīvīs _____   6. in dīvitiīs _____

2. in lōdīce _____   7. in itinere _____

3. in equō _____   8. cum familiā _____

4. cum fidē _____   9. in gladiō _____

5. cum vīnō _____   10. cum arcīs _____

G. Translate these prepositional phrases into Latin.

1. in the sky _____   6. with cake _____

2. with joy _____   7. on ice _____

3. with a legion _____   8. in a turret _____

4. on the roof _____   9. in the races _____

5. with the monkeys _____   10. with a fox _____

H. These prepositional phrases include adjectives. Translate them into English.

1. in proeliō horrendō _____

2. in maribus caeruleīs _____

3. rotundō cum cāseō _____

4. generōsō cum corde _____

5. in lūcīs obscūrīs _____

I. These sentences all use prepositions. Underline each preposition and its object (and any adjective modifying the object), and translate the sentences into English.

1. Senex in insulā calidā hiemābit. _____

_____

2. Agricola mīrus camēlopardalēs in agrīs tenuit. _____

_____

3. Puella avī in fenestrā arcanum dīxit. _____

_____

4. Iūdicēs latrōnem suspīciōsīs cum oculīs spectant. _____

_____

5. Famulae lōdīcēs pulvereās magnā cum virtūte pulsābant! _____

_____

6. Virum rubrīs cum crepidīs nōn dēcipiēs. _____

_____

7. Custōs generōsus captīvum in turre hilarāvit. _____

_____

8. Mūrēs grātī in urbe cum familiā hiemāvērunt. _____

_____

9. Vir per forum suspīciōsā cum arcā ambulābat. _____

_____

10. Nuntius in nāve stetit et ad mare longinquum spectāvit. _____

_____

Translate these sentences into Latin.

11. The secret is safe with me! _____

12. The cat is sleeping in a blanket on the chair. _____

13. The king has dust in an eye. _____

14. We keep the blankets in the brown chest. _____

15. I saw a mouse on the table with the flowers! _____

_____

J. Give a synopsis for each of the following verbs.

1. *hiemō* in the second person singular:_____

	LATIN	ENGLISH
PRESENT ACT.		
FUTURE ACT.		
IMPERFECT ACT.		
PERFECT ACT.		

2. *teneō* in the first person plural: _____

	LATIN	ENGLISH
PRESENT ACT.		
FUTURE ACT.		
IMPERFECT ACT.		
PERFECT ACT.		

3. *hilarō* in the third person plural: _____

	LATIN	ENGLISH
PRESENT ACT.		
FUTURE ACT.		
IMPERFECT ACT.		
PERFECT ACT.		

4. *dēcipiō* in the third person singular: _____

	LATIN	ENGLISH
PRESENT ACT.		
FUTURE ACT.		
IMPERFECT ACT.		
PERFECT ACT.		

K. Give a derivative for each of these verbs.

1. dēcipiō _____   2. teneō _____

L. Answer the following questions about this week's quotation.

1. What does *cum laude* mean? _____

2. What part of speech is *cum*? _____

3. What is the gender, number, and case of *laude*? _____

4. *Laude* is the _____ of *cum*.

WEEK 29

Word List

NOUNS

1. būtūrum, -ī (n) . . . . butter
2. carō, carnis (f) . . . . meat, flesh
3. condīmentum, -ī (n) . . . . . . spice, seasoning
4. farīna, -ae (f) . . . . flour
5. ōvum, -ī (n) . . . . egg
6. piper, piperis (n) . . . . pepper
7. sacchārum, -ī (n) . . . . sugar
8. sāl, salis (m) . . . . salt, wit
9. ūva, -ae (f) . . . . grape

ADJECTIVES

10. meus, -a, -um . . . . my, mine
11. noster, nostra, nostrum . . . our, ours
12. tuus, -a, -um . . . . your, yours (sing.)
13. vester, vestra, vestrum . . . your, yours (pl.)

VERBS

14. agō, agere, ēgī, actum . . . . I do, act
15. coquō, coquere, coxī, coctum . . . . I cook, bake

PREPOSITIONS

16. sine (with abl.) . . . . without

Chant:

No new chant this week.

Quotation:

cum grānō salis—"with a grain of salt"

Weekly Worksheet 29

name:

A. Give a synopsis for each of the following verbs.

1. *coquō* in the first person plural: _____

	LATIN	ENGLISH
PRESENT ACT.		
FUTURE ACT.		
IMPERFECT ACT.		
PERFECT ACT.		

2. *gustō* in the third person singular: _____

	LATIN	ENGLISH
PRESENT ACT.		
FUTURE ACT.		
IMPERFECT ACT.		
PERFECT ACT.		

3. *agō* in the second person singular: _____

	LATIN	ENGLISH
PRESENT ACT.		
FUTURE ACT.		
IMPERFECT ACT.		
PERFECT ACT.		

B. For each noun, give its gender, base, and singular and plural ablative forms.

	NOUN	GENDER	BASE	SINGULAR ABLATIVE	PLURAL ABLATIVE
1.	pepper				
2.	meat				
3.	grape				
4.	spice				
5.	cow				
6.	egg				
7.	flour				
8.	salt				
9.	apple				
10.	sugar				
11.	ice				
12.	butter				

C. Label each noun's declension (1, 2, 3, 3i, 4, or 5) and gender (M, F, or N), then decline it by adding the correct endings to the noun's base.

DECLENSION _____ GENDER _____

	SINGULAR	PLURAL
NOM.	carō	carn
GEN.	carn	carn
DAT.	carn	carn
ACC.	carn	carn
ABL.	carn	carn

DECLENSION _____ GENDER _____

	SINGULAR	PLURAL
NOM.	piper	piper
GEN.	piper	piper
DAT.	piper	piper
ACC.	piper	piper
ABL.	piper	piper

D. Decline *your (sg.) blanket.*

	SINGULAR	PLURAL
NOM.		
GEN.		
DAT.		
ACC.		
ABL.		

E. Underline all of the nouns that could be in the ablative case.

ūva	dīvitiīs	capitī	salem	manibus	ōvōs
gurgite	cavum	nivium	agrō	mūrēs	vastitātibus
lacuum	sanguine	harēnae	lūcernīs	animālī	cāseus
sacchārō	lōdīcum	oculīs	mēlōnī	caput	latebram

F. Fill in the blanks.

1. A _____ connects a noun or pronoun to the rest of a _____.

2. That noun or pronoun is called the _____ of the _____.

3. The preposition *sine* always takes a noun in the _____ case.

4. The preposition *in* means "_____" when paired with a noun in the accusative case.

5. The preposition *in* means "_____" or "_____" when paired with a noun in the ablative case.

6. A predicate _____ follows a linking verb and identifies or _____ the

subject noun.

7. Which Latin case do you use for this part of speech? _____

G. Answer the following questions about this week's quotation.

1. What does *cum grānō salis* mean?_____

2. The preposition *cum* means "_____" and always takes a noun in the

_____ case.

3. Based on this, which case must *grānō* be? _____

4. What is the gender, number, and case of *salis*? _____

H. Translate these prepositional phrases into English. Underline the ending of the object and any adjectives describing it.

1. sine sacchārō _____

2. in būtūrō _____

3. cum sale _____

4. tuīs cum ōvīs _____

5. sine pulvere _____

6. in carne meā _____

7. rubrīs cum mālīs _____

8. sine condīmentīs _____

9. cum pipere _____

10. sine multō sale _____

I. Translate these prepositional phrases into Latin.

1. without salt _____

2. with great wit _____

3. on my sandals _____

4. in your (sg.) family _____

5. without many riches _____

6. with a suspicious expression _____

7. without a tail _____

8. without much hope _____

J. Answer the following questions about derivatives from this week's Word List. The derivatives are italicized.

1. The English word *oval* comes from the Latin word _____.

2. The shape of an *oval* is like an _____.

3. The English word *salami* comes from the Latin word _____.

4. *Salami* is a type of _____ sausage.

5. The English word *cuisine* comes from the Latin word _____.

6. A *cuisine* is a style of _____.

K. On the lines below, give the Latin word for each picture. (If there is more than one, make the word plural!)

1. _____   2. _____   3. _____   4. _____

5. _____   6. _____   7. _____   8. _____

L. Translate these sentences into English. Underline any prepositional phrases. (Be sure to watch the cases!)

1. In ludō sine sale agere nōn cupiō. _____

_____

2. Mulier placentam mīram sine farīnā fēcit. _____

_____

3. Dux pulverem et maculās in vestibus tuīs vīdit, et nōn erat laetus._____

_____

4. Pater māla, ōva, vel sacchārum in iūs nōn pōnet. _____

_____

5. Mīles canem acūtīs cum auribus et sine caudā emēbat. _____

_____

6. Hospes noster dīxit, "Piper in vīnō gustō!" _____

_____

7. Pinnās et flōrēs in comā meā gerēbam. _____

_____

8. Famulae cum sale in hortō rīdent. _____

_____

9. Cēna erit carō cum būtūrō fungīsque et pānis. _____

_____

10. Hērōs multās labōrēs dūrās cum audāciā et virtūte ēgit, sed patellās purgāre nōn amāvit._____

_____

_____

Translate these sentences into Latin.

11. The red grapes are mine._____

12. The lion without a mane is the mother. _____

13. Did you eat the meat on my plate?_____

_____

14. The girls loved to eat bread with butter. _____

_____

15. Do you all want your (pl.) eggs with or without salt? _____

_____

[This page intentionally blank]

WEEK 30

Word List

NOUNS

1. aestās, aestātis (f) . . . . summer
2. annus, -ī (m) . . . . year
3. autumnus, -ī (m) . . . . autumn, fall
4. hiems, hiemis (f) . . . . winter
5. lux, lūcis (f) . . . . light
6. terra, -ae (f) . . . . earth, land
7. vēr, vēris (n) . . . . spring
8. vesper, vesperis (m) . . . . evening, evening star
9. vespertīliō, vespertīliōnis (m) . . . bat

ADJECTIVES

10. unus, -a, -um . . . . one
11. duo, -ae, -o . . . . two
12. trēs, tria . . . . three
13. quattuor . . . . four
14. quinque . . . . five
15. sex . . . . six
16. septem . . . . seven
17. octō . . . . eight
18. novem . . . . nine
19. decem . . . . ten

VERBS

20. creō (1) . . . . I create

Chant:

Declined Numeral: *duo,* two

	MASCULINE	FEMININE	NEUTER
NOM.	duo	duae	duo
GEN.	duōrum	duārum	duōrum
DAT.	duōbus	duābus	duōbus
ACC.	duōs	duās	duōs
ABL.	duōbus	duābus	duōbus

Declined Numeral: *trēs,* three

	MASC./FEM.	NEUTER
NOM.	trēs	tria
GEN.	trium	trium
DAT.	tribus	tribus
ACC.	trēs	tria
ABL.	tribus	tribus

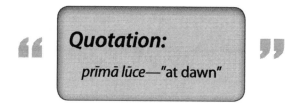

Quotation:

prīmā lūce—"at dawn"

Weekly Worksheet 30

name:

A. Give the singular and plural ablative endings for each declension.

	DECLENSION	SINGULAR ABLATIVE	PLURAL ABLATIVE
1.	first		
2.	second		
3.	second neuter		
4.	third		
5.	third neuter		
6.	third i-stem		
7.	third i-stem neuter		
8.	fourth		
9.	fourth neuter		
10.	fifth		

B. Answer true (T) or false (F) for each statement.

_____ 1. The phrase *prīmā lūce* is in the ablative case.

_____ 2. The phrase *prīmā lūce* is an example of the ablative of time.

_____ 3. The ablative of time does not take a preposition.

_____ 4. The ablative of time always uses a noun related to time, like *noon* or *winter*.

_____ 5. *Nocte* could mean any of the following: *at night, in the night, during the night.*

_____ 6. "During the long night" in Latin would be *nocte longō.*

C. Cross out any noun *not* in the ablative case.

vēre	būtūrum	lōdīcibus	dīvitiīs	ūvā	annōs
coniugibus	rētī	maris	nive	exemplō	rēbus
lūce	terra	vultū	avāritiīs	genūs	harēnae
manuī	capitis	legiōnibus	virtūte	elephantō	vespertīliōnis

D. For each noun, give its base and its singular and plural ablative forms.

	NOUN	BASE	SINGULAR ABLATIVE	PLURAL ABLATIVE
1.	autumn			
2.	light			
3.	bat			
4.	flour			
5.	year			
6.	spring			
7.	evening			
8.	day			
9.	winter			
10.	summer			

E. Each of these phrases uses the ablative of time. Translate them into English, giving as many variations as you can. Two examples are given below.

nocte   *at night, in the night, during the night*

prīmō diē   *on the first day, during the first day, within the first day*

1. aestāte _____

2. vesperibus _____

3. vēre _____

4. hiemibus _____

5. prīmā hieme _____

6. decem diēbus _____

7. octō annīs longīs _____

8. prīmō autumnō_____

F. Translate each of these phrases. All of them will use the ablative of time.

1. during the days _____

2. at the time_____

3. at noon _____

4. in the first summer _____

5. during the cold night _____

6. in one day _____

G. In the charts below, decline the Latin word for *two*, then the Latin word for *three*.

two

	MASCULINE	FEMININE	NEUTER
NOM.			
GEN.			
DAT.			
ACC.			
ABL.			

three

	MASC./FEM.	NEUTER
NOM.		
GEN.		
DAT.		
ACC.		
ABL.		

H. Underline any uses of the ablative of time, then translate these sentences into English.

1. Aestāte in lacum salīre amāmus._____

2. Unam avem in manū meā cupiō, sed duās avēs in arbore cupis. _____

_____

3. Amīcus meus mē prīmā lūce tollet. _____

4. Hieme lux erat obscūra et ventus erat gelidus. _____

_____

5. Coquus nōbīs iūs mīrum tempore creābit._____

_____

6. Dux quattuor nuntiōs trans regiōnem simul mīsit. _____

_____

7. Sex diēbus Deus caelum et terram creāvit._____

_____

8. Octō sīmiae in aedificium per fenestram nocte scandērunt._____

_____

9. Quinque annīs hērōs decem dracōnēs vīcit, quattuor antra magica invēnit, et trēs rēgīnās

conservāvit. _____

_____

10. Vesper nuntium citum per tenebrās dūxit. _____

_____

Translate these sentences into Latin.

11. They will buy grain during the summer. _____

12. One torch was burning during the evening. _____

13. We saw three distant mountains and sea at dawn. _____

_____

14. On the first day, I walked with my father to the city. _____

_____

15. Nine horrible bats flew into the tower during the night! _____

_____

I. Answer the following questions about this week's quotation.

1. What does *prīmā lūce* mean? _____

2. What part of speech is *prīmā?* _____

3. What is the gender, number, and case of *lūce?*_____

4. *Prīmā lūce* is an example of the _____ of time.

J. Give a synopsis for *creō* in the third person singular.

_____

	LATIN	ENGLISH
PRESENT ACT.		
FUTURE ACT.		
IMPERFECT ACT.		
PERFECT ACT.		

K. Use the vocabulary from this week's Word List to complete the definition of these English derivatives.

1. When a bear goes into *hibernation,* she is sleeping through the _____.

    a) concert   b) year   c) winter

2. A *vespertilian* superhero resembles a _____ in some way!

    a) star   b) bat   c) snake

3. A poem made up of _____ lines is called a *quatrain.*

    a) rhyming   b) four   c) many

4. During the first *lunar* landing, American astronauts walked on the _____.

    a) moon   b) sunlight   c) flowers

WEEK 31

Word List

NOUNS

1. domus, -ūs (f) . . . . home, house
2. frāter, frātris (m) . . . . brother
3. hōra, -ae (f) . . . . hour
4. lūna, -ae (f) . . . . moon
5. mensis, mensis (m) . . . . . . month
6. puer, puerī (m) . . . . boy
7. sōl, sōlis (m) . . . . sun
8. soror, sorōris (f) . . . . sister

ADJECTIVES

9. paucī, -ae, -a . . . . few, little
10. secundus, -a, -um . . . . . . second
11. tertius, -a, -um . . . . third
12. quartus, -a, -um . . . . fourth
13. quintus, -a, -um . . . . fifth
14. sextus, -a, -um . . . . sixth
15. septimus, -a, -um . . . . . . seventh
16. octāvus, -a, -um . . . . eighth
17. nōnus, -a, -um . . . . ninth
18. decimus, -a, -um . . . . . . tenth
19. ultimus, -a, -um . . . . last, farthest

ADVERBS

20. stultē . . . . foolishly

Chant:

No new chant this week.

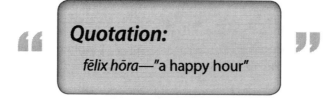

Quotation:

fēlix hōra—"a happy hour"

Weekly Worksheet 31

name:

A. Answer the following questions.

1. Is the ablative of time formed using a preposition? _____

2. Does the ablative of time always use a time-related noun? _____

3. Can the ablative of time be translated in different ways? _____

4. Why is the quotation *prīmā lūce* an example of the ablative of time? _____

_____

4. Could *diē* be an example of the ablative of time? Why or why not? _____

_____

5. Give three possible translations of *diē:* _____

_____

6. Could *mensis* be an example of the ablative of time? Why or why not? _____

_____

B. For each noun, give its base, gender (M, F, or N), declension (1, 2, 3, 3i, 4, or 5), and translation.

	NOUN	BASE	GENDER	DECLENSION	TRANSLATION
1.	soror				
2.	vulpēs				
3.	nāsus				
4.	hōra				
5.	puer				
6.	lūna				

	NOUN	BASE	GENDER	DECLENSION	TRANSLATION
7.	frāter				
8.	vallēs				
9.	mensis				
10.	sōl				
11.	domus				
12.	scopulus				

C. Give the singular and plural ablative endings for each declension.

	DECLENSION	SINGULAR ABLATIVE	PLURAL ABLATIVE
1.	first		
2.	second		
3.	second neuter		
4.	third		
5.	third neuter		
6.	third i-stem		
7.	third i-stem neuter		
8.	fourth		
9.	fourth neuter		
10.	fifth		

D. Each of these phrases uses the ablative of time. Translate them into English, giving as many variations as you can. An example is given below.

quintā hōrā   *at the fifth hour, during the fifth hour, in the fifth hour*

1. mense _____

2. hōrā _____

3. vespere _____

4. nōnō annō _____

5. tertiō diē _____

6. paucīs mensibus _____

7. paucīs hōrīs _____

8. ultimō diē _____

E. Translate each of these phrases. All of them will use the ablative of time.

1. within two hours _____

2. on the fifth day _____

3. in the last month _____

4. during a few years _____

5. in the second winter _____

6. at the last hour _____

F. Give a synopsis for each of the following verbs.

1. *gustō* in the third person plural: _____

	LATIN	ENGLISH
PRESENT ACT.		
FUTURE ACT.		
IMPERFECT ACT.		
PERFECT ACT.		

2. *gerō* in the first person singular: _____

	LATIN	ENGLISH
PRESENT ACT.		
FUTURE ACT.		
IMPERFECT ACT.		
PERFECT ACT.		

3. *sedeō* in the third person singular: _____

	LATIN	ENGLISH
PRESENT ACT.		
FUTURE ACT.		
IMPERFECT ACT.		
PERFECT ACT.		

G. Decline the phrase *second month*.

	SINGULAR	PLURAL
NOM.		
GEN.		
DAT.		
ACC.		
ABL.		

H. Use the vocabulary from this week's Word List to complete the definition of these English derivatives.

1. If there is a *paucity* of food, it means there is only _____ food.

a) reptile's   b) a little   c) hourly

2. A *nonagon* is a shape with _____ sides.

    a) curved   b) no   c) nine

3. A *semester* is a school term made up of six _____.

    a) hours   b) days   c) months

4. A *quart* is one _____ of a gallon.

    a) third   b) fourth   c) fifth

I. Underline any uses of the ablative of time, then translate these sentences into English.

1. Dominus tertiō diē iterum surrēxit._____

2. Sextā hōrā hōrologium nōn sonuit. _____

_____

3. Frāter meus placentam ante cēnam stultē ēdit._____

_____

4. Virī fīdī hostēs decimō diē vīcērunt. _____

_____

5. Puer callidus volābit et prīmum pīrātam sine misericordiā oppugnābit._____

_____

6. Lūcetne lūna nostra sōlum nocte? _____

_____

7. Soror mea ad oppidum paucīs diēbus venit. _____

_____

8. Paucīs hōrīs sine quattuor ōvīs placentam creāre nōn possum. _____

_____

9. Nuntius fessus comitī facem litterāsque nocte dedit. _____

_____

10. Merīdiē trēs explōrātōrēs in fluviō paucōs crocodīlōs stultē pugnābat. _____

_____

_____

Translate these sentences into Latin.

11. The sun is high in the sky at noon. _____

12. On the sixth day, God created animals and a man and a woman._____

_____

13. New snow cheered up the children during the long winter. _____

_____

14. On the eighth day, my hair was a horrible disaster! _____

_____

15. I have seven brothers, and I am the third._____

_____

J. Answer the following questions about this week's quotation.

1. What does *fēlix hōra* mean? _____

2. What is the gender, number, and case of *hōra?* _____

3. What part of speech is the word *fēlix?* _____

4. An adjective must always match the noun it describes in _____, _____,

and _____.

5. What then is the gender, number, and case of *fēlix?* _____

WEEK 32

Word List

NOUNS

1. corōna, -ae (f) . . . . crown
2. error, errōris (m) . . . . error, mistake

ADJECTIVES

3. dexter, dextra, dextrum . . . . . . right, proper
4. sinister, sinistra, sinistrum . . . . . left, wrong

Chant:

No new chant this week.

Quotation:

No new quotation this week.

[This page intentionally blank]

Weekly Worksheet 32   *name:* _____

A. Fill in the blanks.

1. A _____ connects a _____ or pronoun to the rest of a sentence.

2. That noun or pronoun is called the _____ of the _____.

3. *Prepositional phrase* is another name for a _____ and its object (and any modifiers).

B. Draw a line to connect the preposition to the case its object takes.

1. trans

2. in ("in, on")

3. ad   **ACCUSATIVE**

4. post

5. cum

6. ante

7. propter   **ABLATIVE**

8. in ("into")

9. sine

10. per

C. Translate these prepositional phrases into English. Underline the ending of the object.

1. cum corōnā _____

2. per errōrem _____

3. in domū _____

4. sine lūce _____

5. propter arcana _____

6. post aestātem _____

7. in arcās _____

8. ad castellum _____

9. trans palūdēs _____

10. ante hiemem _____

D. Answer true (T) or false (F) for each statement.

_____ 1. The ablative of time sometimes takes a preposition.

_____ 2. The ablative of time will sometimes be in the accusative.

_____ 3. *Hōrā* could mean any of the following: *in an hour, on the hour, within an hour.*

_____ 4. The phrase *prīmā lūce* is an example of the ablative of time.

_____ 5. The ablative of time always uses a noun related to time, like *day* or *month.*

_____ 6. In Latin, the phrase "in the third year" would be *tertiō annō.*

_____ 7. The ablative of time cannot include adjectives.

E. Each of these phrases uses the ablative of time. Translate them into English, and give at least two translations for each phrase.

1. secundō mense _____

2. paucīs hōrīs _____

3. sex annīs _____

4. nocte _____

5. decimō diē_____

6. vēre _____

7. aestāte sērā _____

8. tempore sinistrō _____

F. Translate each of these phrases. All of them will use the ablative of time.

1. in the first winter _____

2. on the last day_____

3. during the good years _____

4. at the right time _____

5. in seven hours _____

G. For each of the following verbs, give its conjugation and family, then provide a synopsis of it.

1. *amō:* _____ conjugation, "_____" family

2. *amō* in the first person singular:_____

	LATIN	ENGLISH
PRESENT ACT.		
FUTURE ACT.		
IMPERFECT ACT.		
PERFECT ACT.		

3. *videō:* _____ conjugation, "_____" family

4. *videō* in the second person singular: _____

	LATIN	ENGLISH
PRESENT ACT.		
FUTURE ACT.		
IMPERFECT ACT.		
PERFECT ACT.		

5. *dūcō:* _____ conjugation, "_____" family

6. *dūcō* in the third person singular:_____

	LATIN	ENGLISH
PRESENT ACT.		
FUTURE ACT.		
IMPERFECT ACT.		
PERFECT ACT.		

7. *capiō:* _____ conjugation _____, "_____" family

8. *capiō* in the first person plural: _____

	LATIN	ENGLISH
PRESENT ACT.		
FUTURE ACT.		
IMPERFECT ACT.		
PERFECT ACT.		

9. *audiō:* _____ conjugation, "_____" family

10. *audiō* in the third person plural: _____

	LATIN	ENGLISH
PRESENT ACT.		
FUTURE ACT.		
IMPERFECT ACT.		
PERFECT ACT.		

H. Fill in the principal parts. In the parentheses at the end of the line, write which conjugation each verb is in (1, 2, 3, 3io, 4, or 5).

1. creō, _____, _____, _____ (_____)

2. _____, coquere, _____, _____ (_____)

3. teneō, _____, _____, _____ (_____)

4. _____, _____, _____, actum (_____)

5. pulsō, _____, _____, _____ (_____)

6. pōnō, _____, _____, _____ (_____)

7. veniō, _____, _____, _____ (_____)

8. _____, dēcipere, _____, _____ (_____)

9. nuntiō, _____, _____, _____ (_____)

10. _____, secāre, _____, _____ (_____)

11. accūsō, _____, _____, _____ (_____)

12. gustō, _____, _____, _____ (_____)

13. _____, _____, _____, statum (_____)

14. tollō, _____, _____, _____ (_____)

15. hilarō, _____, _____, _____ (_____)

I. Label each noun's declension (1, 2, 3, 3i, 4, or 5) and gender (M, F, or N). Then decline it.

DECLENSION _____ GENDER _____

	SINGULAR	PLURAL
NOM.	error	
GEN.		
DAT.		
ACC.		
ABL.		

DECLENSION _____ GENDER _____

	SINGULAR	PLURAL
NOM.	corōna	
GEN.		
DAT.		
ACC.		
ABL.		

DECLENSION _____ GENDER _____

	SINGULAR	PLURAL
NOM.	manus	
GEN.		
DAT.		
ACC.		
ABL.		

DECLENSION _____ GENDER _____

	SINGULAR	PLURAL
NOM.	puer	
GEN.		
DAT.		
ACC.		
ABL.		

J. Decline *left side.*

	SINGULAR	PLURAL
NOM.		
GEN.		
DAT.		
ACC.		
ABL.		

K. Translate the Latin words into English, and the English words into Latin.

1. brother _____

2. lux _____

3. condīmentum _____

4. wealth _____

5. sagitta _____

6. vallum _____

7. virtūs _____

8. head _____

9. wheel _____

10. culmen _____

11. feast _____

12. lūcus _____

13. cauda _____

14. verū _____

15. crepida _____

16. shield _____

17. līmen _____

18. mēlo _____

19. dust _____

20. famēs _____

21. millstone _____

22. sister _____

23. sōl _____

24. carō _____

25. vespertīliō _____

26. box _____

27. pepper _____

28. sāl _____

L. Complete the Latin quotations, and give the English meaning of each.

1. _____ hoc ergō _____ hoc: _____

2. _____ laude: _____

3. prīmā _____: _____

4. in mediās _____: _____

5. fēlix _____: _____

M. Translate these sentences into English.

1. Puella propter vespertīliōnem in comā meā clāmābat. _____

_____

2. Per errōrem corōna sinistra in capite meō erat. _____

_____

3. Māter vestra dīxit, "Capite viam in latere dextrā." _____

_____

4. Cunīculus famēlicus cavum in hortum fōdit et holera nostra nunc edit! _____

_____

5. Vēre senex lacum et laurōs per fenestram vidēre potest. _____

_____

6. Reus iūdicī sevērō stultē dīxit, "Sinister et ignārus es." _____

_____

7. Sīmiae paucās ariēnās in arboribus hieme invenīre sōlum possunt. _____

_____

8. Secundō diē rēgīna arcam et rem horrendam in mare iēcit. _____

_____

9. Trēs custōdēs cum canibus trans agrum ad captīvum cucurrērunt. _____

_____

10. Leō in urbem errāvit, et nunc hominēs in viīs nōn ambulant. _____

_____

Translate these English sentences into Latin.

11. The lion and the unicorn were fighting because of the crown. _____

_____

12. The quick brother was carrying a warm blanket toward the little sister. _____

_____

13. The man quickly urged the horse through the river. _____

_____

14. Within two months, the new general will win over the experienced soldiers. _____

_____

15. The children loved the wild games, but the mothers loved the quiet games. _____

_____

N. Match each English derivative with its Latin root. On the lines, give the meaning of each Latin word.

1. manacles   corōna _____

2. stable   cauda _____

3. semester   dexter _____

4. ambidextrous   stō _____

5. incarnate   manus _____

6. melon   veniō _____

7. coronation   trahō _____

8. adventure   mensis _____

9. coward   mēlo _____

10. tractor   carō _____

[This page intentionally blank]

APPENDICES

- Chant Charts
- Glossaries
- Sources and Helps

CHANT CHARTS

Chants, in Order of Introduction

The chants in this section appear in the order they are introduced in this book.

Present Active Verb Endings

(Week 1, p. 5)

	SINGULAR	PLURAL		SINGULAR	PLURAL
1ST	-ō	-mus		I am *verbing*, I *verb*	we are *verbing*
2ND	-s	-tis		you are *verbing*	you all are *verbing*
3RD	-t	-nt		he/she/it is *verbing*	they are *verbing*

Future Active Verb Endings

(Week 1, p. 5)

	SINGULAR	PLURAL		SINGULAR	PLURAL
1ST	-bō	-bimus		I will *verb*	we will *verb*
2ND	-bis	-bitis		you will *verb*	you all will *verb*
3RD	-bit	-bunt		he/she/it will *verb*	they will *verb*

Imperfect Active Verb Endings

(Week 1, p. 5)

	SINGULAR	PLURAL		SINGULAR	PLURAL
1ST	-bam	-bāmus		I was *verbing*	we were *verbing*
2ND	-bās	-bātis		you were *verbing*	you all were *verbing*
3RD	-bat	-bant		he/she/it was *verbing*	they were *verbing*

Example of Third Conjugation Verb, *Dūcō*

PRESENT

	SINGULAR	PLURAL
1ST	dūcō	dūcimus
2ND	dūcis	dūcitis
3RD	dūcit	dūcunt

FUTURE

SINGULAR	PLURAL
dūcam	dūcēmus
dūcēs	dūcētis
dūcet	dūcent

IMPERFECT

SINGULAR	PLURAL
dūcēbam	dūcēbāmus
dūcēbās	dūcēbātis
dūcēbat	dūcēbant

Present Active of *Possum* (Irregular Verb)

(Week 2, p. 14)

	SINGULAR	PLURAL		SINGULAR	PLURAL
1ST	possum	possumus		I am able	we are able
2ND	potes	potestis		you are able	you all are able
3RD	potest	possunt		he/she/it is able	they are able

First Declension Noun Endings

(Week 3, p. 20)

	SINGULAR	PLURAL		SINGULAR	PLURAL
NOM.	-a	-ae		a, the *noun*	the *nouns*
GEN.	-ae	-ārum		of the *noun*, the *noun's*	of the *nouns*, the *nouns'*
DAT.	-ae	-īs		to, for the *noun*	to, for the *nouns*
ACC.	-am	-ās		the *noun*	the *nouns*
ABL.	-ā	-īs		by, with, from the *noun*	by, with, from the *nouns*

Second Declension Noun Endings

(Week 3, p. 20)

	SINGULAR	PLURAL		SINGULAR	PLURAL
NOM.	-us	-ī		a, the *noun*	the *nouns*
GEN.	-ī	-ōrum		of the *noun*, the *noun's*	of the *nouns*, the *nouns'*
DAT.	-ō	-īs		to, for the *noun*	to, for the *nouns*
ACC.	-um	-ōs		the *noun*	the *nouns*
ABL.	-ō	-īs		by, with, from the *noun*	by, with, from the *nouns*

Second Declension Neuter Noun Endings

(Week 3, p. 20)

	SINGULAR	PLURAL		SINGULAR	PLURAL
NOM.	-um	-a		a, the *noun*	the *nouns*
GEN.	-ī	-ōrum		of the *noun*, the *noun's*	of the *nouns*, the *nouns'*
DAT.	-ō	-īs		to, for the *noun*	to, for the *nouns*
ACC.	-um	-a		the *noun*	the *nouns*
ABL.	-ō	-īs		by, with, from the *noun*	by, with, from the *nouns*

Third Declension Noun Endings
(Week 4, p. 28)

	SINGULAR	PLURAL		SINGULAR	PLURAL
NOM.	**x**	-ēs		a, the *noun*	the *nouns*
GEN.	-is	-um		of the *noun*, the *noun's*	of the *nouns*, the *nouns'*
DAT.	-ī	-ibus		to, for the *noun*	to, for the *nouns*
ACC.	-em	-ēs		the *noun*	the *nouns*
ABL.	-e	-ibus		by, with, from the *noun*	by, with, from the *nouns*

Third Declension Neuter Noun Endings
(Week 4, p. 28)

	SINGULAR	PLURAL		SINGULAR	PLURAL
NOM.	**x**	-a		a, the *noun*	the *nouns*
GEN.	-is	-um		of the *noun*, the *noun's*	of the *nouns*, the *nouns'*
DAT.	-ī	-ibus		to, for the *noun*	to, for the *nouns*
ACC.	**x**	-a		the *noun*	the *nouns*
ABL.	-e	-ibus		by, with, from the *noun*	by, with, from the *nouns*

Fourth Declension Noun Endings
(Week 4, p. 28)

	SINGULAR	PLURAL		SINGULAR	PLURAL
NOM.	-us	-ūs		a, the *noun*	the *nouns*
GEN.	-ūs	-uum		of the *noun*, the *noun's*	of the *nouns*, the *nouns'*
DAT.	-uī	-ibus		to, for the *noun*	to, for the *nouns*
ACC.	-um	-ūs		the *noun*	the *nouns*
ABL.	-ū	-ibus		by, with, from the *noun*	by, with, from the *nouns*

Fourth Declension Neuter Noun Endings
(Week 4, p. 29)

	SINGULAR	PLURAL		SINGULAR	PLURAL
NOM.	-ū	-ua		a, the *noun*	the *nouns*
GEN.	-ūs	-uum		of the *noun*, the *noun's*	of the *nouns*, the *nouns'*
DAT.	-ū	-ibus		to, for the *noun*	to, for the *nouns*
ACC.	-ū	-ua		the *noun*	the *nouns*
ABL.	-ū	-ibus		by, with, from the *noun*	by, with, from the *nouns*

Present Active of *Sum* (Irregular Verb)
(Week 5, p. 36)

	SINGULAR	PLURAL		SINGULAR	PLURAL
1ST	sum	sumus		I am	we are
2ND	es	estis		you are	you all are
3RD	est	sunt		he/she/it is	they are

Future Active of *Sum* (Irregular Verb)
(Week 5, p. 36)

	SINGULAR	PLURAL		SINGULAR	PLURAL
1ST	erō	erimus		I will be	we will be
2ND	eris	eritis		you will be	you all will be
3RD	erit	erunt		he/she/it will be	they will be

Imperfect Active of *Sum* (Irregular Verb)
(Week 5, p. 36)

	SINGULAR	PLURAL		SINGULAR	PLURAL
1ST	eram	erāmus		I was	we were
2ND	erās	erātis		you were	you all were
3RD	erat	erant		he/she/it was	they were

Third Declension i-Stem Noun Endings: Masculine & Feminine
(Week 9, p. 74)

	SINGULAR	PLURAL		SINGULAR	PLURAL
NOM.	x	-ēs		a, the *noun*	the *nouns*
GEN.	-is	-ium		of the *noun*, the *noun's*	of the *nouns*, the *nouns'*
DAT.	-ī	-ibus		to, for the *noun*	to, for the *nouns*
ACC.	-em	-ēs		the *noun*	the *nouns*
ABL.	-e	-ibus		by, with, from the *noun*	by, with, from the *nouns*

Third Declension i-Stem Noun Endings: Neuter
(Week 10, p. 82)

	SINGULAR	PLURAL		SINGULAR	PLURAL
NOM.	x	-ia		a, the *noun*	the *nouns*
GEN.	-is	-ium		of the *noun*, the *noun's*	of the *nouns*, the *nouns'*
DAT.	-ī	-ibus		to, for the *noun*	to, for the *nouns*
ACC.	x	-ia		the *noun*	the *nouns*
ABL.	-ī	-ibus		by, with, from the *noun*	by, with, from the *nouns*

Fifth Declension Noun Endings

(Week 12, p. 104)

	SINGULAR	PLURAL		SINGULAR	PLURAL
NOM.	-ēs	-ēs		a, the *noun*	the *nouns*
GEN.	-ēī / -eī	-ērum		of the *noun*, the *noun's*	of the *nouns*, the *nouns'*
DAT.	-ēī / -eī	-ēbus		to, for the *noun*	to, for the *nouns*
ACC.	-em	-ēs		the *noun*	the *nouns*
ABL.	-ē	-ēbus		by, with, from the *noun*	by, with, from the *nouns*

Personal Pronouns: *ego, nōs*

(Week 14, p. 120)

	SINGULAR	PLURAL		SINGULAR	PLURAL
NOM.	ego	nōs		I	we
GEN.	meī	nostrum		of me	of us
DAT.	mihi	nōbīs		to, for me	to, for us
ACC.	mē	nōs		me	us
ABL.	mē	nōbīs		by, with, from me	by, with, from us

Personal Pronouns: *tū, vōs*

(Week 14, p. 120)

	SINGULAR	PLURAL		SINGULAR	PLURAL
NOM.	tū	vōs		you	you all
GEN.	tuī	vestrum		of you	of you all
DAT.	tibi	vōbīs		to, for you	to, for you all
ACC.	tē	vōs		you	you all
ABL.	tē	vōbīs		by, with, from you	by, with, from you all

Present Active of *Audiō*, Fourth Conjugation Verb

(Week 17, p. 148)

	SINGULAR	PLURAL		SINGULAR	PLURAL
1ST	audiō	audīmus		I hear	we hear
2ND	audīs	audītis		you hear	you all hear
3RD	audit	audiunt		he/she/it hears	they hear

Future Active of *Audiō*
(Week 17, p. 148)

	SINGULAR	PLURAL		SINGULAR	PLURAL
1ST	audiam	audiēmus		I will hear	we will hear
2ND	audiēs	audiētis		you will hear	you all will hear
3RD	audiet	audient		he/she/it will hear	they will hear

Imperfect Active of *Audiō*
(Week 17, p. 148)

	SINGULAR	PLURAL		SINGULAR	PLURAL
1ST	audiēbam	audiēbāmus		I was hearing	we were hearing
2ND	audiēbās	audiēbātis		you were hearing	you all were hearing
3RD	audiēbat	audiēbant		he/she/it was hearing	they were hearing

Present Active of *Capiō*, Third Conjugation *-iō* Verb
(Week 18, p. 156)

	SINGULAR	PLURAL		SINGULAR	PLURAL
1ST	capiō	capimus		I take	we take
2ND	capis	capitis		you take	you all take
3RD	capit	capiunt		he/she/it takes	they take

Future Active of *Capiō*
(Week 18, p. 156)

	SINGULAR	PLURAL		SINGULAR	PLURAL
1ST	capiam	capiēmus		I will take	we will take
2ND	capiēs	capiētis		you will take	you all will take
3RD	capiet	capient		he/she/it will take	they will take

Imperfect Active of *Capiō*
(Week 18, p. 156)

	SINGULAR	PLURAL		SINGULAR	PLURAL
1ST	capiēbam	capiēbāmus		I was taking	we were taking
2ND	capiēbās	capiēbātis		you were taking	you all were taking
3RD	capiēbat	capiēbant		he/she/it was taking	they were taking

Perfect Active Verb Endings

(Week 20, p. 174)

	SINGULAR	PLURAL		SINGULAR	PLURAL
1ST	-ī	-imus		I *verbed,* have *verbed*	we *verbed*
2ND	-istī	-istis		you *verbed*	you all *verbed*
3RD	-it	-ērunt		he/she/it *verbed*	they *verbed*

Declined Numeral: *duo,* two

(Week 30, p. 266)

	MASCULINE	FEMININE	NEUTER
NOM.	duo	duae	duo
GEN.	duōrum	duārum	duōrum
DAT.	duōbus	duābus	duōbus
ACC.	duōs	duās	duōs
ABL.	duōbus	duābus	duōbus

Declined Numeral: *trēs,* three

(Week 30, p. 266)

	MASC./FEM.	NEUTER
NOM.	trēs	tria
GEN.	trium	trium
DAT.	tribus	tribus
ACC.	trēs	tria
ABL.	tribus	tribus

Verb Chants, applied to amō, videō, dūcō, capiō, and audiō

The chants in this section follow the conjugations of amō *(1st) ,* videō *(2nd),* dūcō *(3rd)* capiō *(3rd -iō), and* audiō *(4th) through the present, future, imperfect, and perfect tenses. Endings have been bolded.*

	1ST	2ND	3RD	3RD -IŌ	4TH
PRESENT	am**ō**	vid**eō**	dūc**ō**	capi**ō**	audi**ō**
	am**ās**	vid**ēs**	dūc**is**	cap**is**	aud**īs**
	am**at**	vid**et**	dūc**it**	cap**it**	aud**it**
	am**āmus**	vid**ēmus**	dūc**imus**	cap**imus**	aud**īmus**
	am**ātis**	vid**ētis**	dūc**itis**	cap**itis**	aud**ītis**
	am**ant**	vid**ent**	dūc**unt**	cap**iunt**	aud**iunt**

	1ST	2ND	3RD	3RD -IŌ	4TH
FUTURE	amā**bō**	vidē**bō**	dūc**am**	capi**am**	audi**am**
	amā**bis**	vidē**bis**	dūc**ēs**	capi**ēs**	audi**ēs**
	amā**bit**	vidē**bit**	dūc**et**	capi**et**	audi**et**
	amā**bimus**	vidē**bimus**	dūc**ēmus**	capi**ēmus**	audi**ēmus**
	amā**bitis**	vidē**bitis**	dūc**ētis**	capi**ētis**	audi**ētis**
	amā**bunt**	vidē**bunt**	dūc**ent**	capi**ent**	audi**ent**

	1ST	2ND	3RD	3RD -IŌ	4TH
IMPERFECT	amā**bam**	vidē**bam**	dūcē**bam**	capiē**bam**	audiē**bam**
	amā**bās**	vidē**bās**	dūcē**bās**	capiē**bās**	audiē**bās**
	amā**bat**	vidē**bat**	dūcē**bat**	capiē**bat**	audiē**bat**
	amā**bāmus**	vidē**bāmus**	dūcē**bāmus**	capiē**bāmus**	audiē**bāmus**
	amā**bātis**	vidē**bātis**	dūcē**bātis**	capiē**bātis**	audiē**bātis**
	amā**bant**	vidē**bant**	dūcē**bant**	capiē**bant**	audiē**bant**

	1ST	2ND	3RD	3RD -IŌ	4TH
PERFECT	amāv**ī**	vīd**ī**	dūx**ī**	cēp**ī**	audīv**ī**
	amā**vistī**	vīd**istī**	dūx**istī**	cēp**istī**	audī**vistī**
	amāv**it**	vīd**it**	dūx**it**	cēp**it**	audīv**it**
	amā**vimus**	vīd**imus**	dūx**imus**	cēp**imus**	audī**vimus**
	amā**vistis**	vīd**istis**	dūx**istis**	cēp**istis**	audī**vistis**
	amāv**ērunt**	vīd**ērunt**	dūx**ērunt**	cēp**ērunt**	audīv**ērunt**

ENGLISH-LATIN GLOSSARY

When using any English-Latin glossary, always keep in mind that these two languages don't always mesh perfectly. For example, if you look up "little" you will find both *parvus* and *paucī*. They both can mean "little," but you'll have to use good judgment to decide which is correct in a given context!

Also, most English-Latin glossaries don't provide you with every bit of information about a noun—they are simply tools to help you in the right direction. This one is the same. It won't give you a noun's genitive singular form or gender, but it will give you the information you need to find those things out!

A

accelerate, *properō*

accept, *accipiō*

accuse, *accūsō*

across, *trans (with acc.)*

act, *agō*

advertise, *vendō*

after, *post (with acc.)*

again, *iterum*

agreeable, *grātus*

ally, *socius*

almost, *paene*

alone, *sōlus*

always, *semper*

am, *sum*

am able, *possum*

am acceptable to,
  placeō

am bright, *lūceō*

am concealed, *lateō*

am mistaken, *errō*

am on guard against,
  caveō

am wary of, *caveō*

am white, *candeō*

am worthy of, *mereō*

amusing, *rīdiculus*

and, *et, -que*

angry, *īrātus*

animal, *animal*

announce, *nuntiō*

annoy, *vexō*

anxious, *trepidus*

ape, *sīmia*

apple, *mālum*

approach, *appropinquō*

arch, *arcus*

architect, *architectus*

area, *regiō*

arm, *brācchium*

army, *exercitus*

arouse, *agitō*

arrow, *sagitta*

ashes, *cinis*

ask, *rogō*

associate, *socius*

at the same time, *simul*

athletic field, *campus*

attack, *oppugnō*

authority, *auctōritās*

autumn, *autumnus*

avoid, *vītō*

awful, *horrendus*

axe, *secūris*

B

bacon, *lardum*

bad, *malus*

badger, *mēlēs*

bake, *coquō*

banana, *ariēna*

bat, *vespertīliō*

battle, *proelium*

be, *sum*

be able, *possum*

be acceptable to,
  placeō

be bright, *lūceō*

be concealed, *lateō*

be mistaken, *errō*

be on guard against,
  caveō

be wary of, *caveō*

be white, *candeō*

be worthy of, *mereō*

beach, *lītus*

bear (v.), *gerō*

beat, *pulsō, vincō*

beautiful, *pulcher*

because of, *propter*
  (with acc.)

bed, *lectus*

before, *ante (with acc.)*

behind, *post (with acc.)*

bellow, *rudō*

beloved, *cārus*

big, *magnus*

bird, *avis*

bite, *mordeō*

bitter, *acerbus*

black, *niger*

blame (v.), *accūsō*

blame (n.), *culpa*

blanket, *lōdix*

blaze, *ardeō*

blond, *flāvus*

blood, *sanguis*

blue, *caeruleus*

bog, *palūs*

boldness, *audācia*

bow, *arcus*

box, *arca*

boy, *puer*

bray, *rudō*

bread, *pānis*

break, *frangō*

bridge, *pōns*

bright, *clārus*

brother, *frāter*

brown, *brūnus*

build, *faciō*

building, *aedificium, tectum*

bull, *bōs*

burden, *onus*

burn, *ardeō, torreō*

but, *sed*

butter, *būtūrum*

buy, *emō*

C

cake, *placenta*

call, *vocō*

call together, *convocō*

can, *possum*

captive, *captīvus*

capture, *capiō*

carry, *portō, vehō*

cart, *carrus*

castle, *castellum*

cat, *fēlēs*

catch, *capiō*

cave, *antrum*

chair, *sella*

change, *mūtō*

chant, *carmen*

cheer up, *hilarō*

cheese, *cāseus*

chef, *coquus*

chest, *arca*

children, *līberī*

chill, *gelū*

circular, *rotundus*

citizen, *cīvis*

city, *urbs*

claw, *unguis*

clean, *purgō*

cleanse, *purgō*

clear (adj.), *clārus*

clear (v.), *purgō*

clever, *callidus*

cliff, *scopulus*

climb, *scandō*

clock, *hōrologium*

clothing, *vestis*

cold, *gelidus*

colonist, *incola*

come, *veniō*

come together, *conveniō*

come upon, *inveniō*

command, *mandō*

companion, *comes, socius*

condemn, *damnō*

conquer, *vincō*

constellation, *astrum*

continue, *pergō*

convey, *vehō*

cook (n.), *coquus*

cook (v.), *coquō*

couch, *lectus*

cough, *tussiō*

courage, *audācia, virtūs*

cow, *bōs*

cowboy, *armentārius*

crag, *scopulus*

create, *creō*

crime, *dēlictum*

crocodile, *crocodīlus*

crops, *frūmentum (pl.)*

crowd, *caterva*

crown, *corōna*

cunning, *callidus*

curious, *cūriōsus*

cut, *secō*

D

damp, *ūmidus*

danger, *perīculum*

dark, *obscūrus, niger*

darkness, *tenebrae*

day, *diēs*

dear, *cārus*

deceive, *dēcipiō*

decision, *sententia*

declare, *dēclārō*

deer, *cervus*

defeat, *vincō*

defendant, *reus*

delay, *tardō*

delight, *dēlectō*

demand, *postulō*

dense, *densus*

dentist, *medicus*

desert, *vastitās*

deserve, *mereō*

destiny, *fātum*

destruction, *cinis, perniciēs*

die, *occidō*

difficult, *dūrus*

difficulties, *angustiae*

dig, *fodiō*

diligent, *cūriōsus*

dinner, *cēna*

direction, *regiō*

disaster, *perniciēs*

discover, *inveniō*

dish, *patella*

distant, *longinquus*

disturb, *agitō*

do, *agō, faciō*

doctor, *medicus*

dog, *canis*

doorway, *līmen*

drag, *trahō*

dragon, *dracō*

draw, *trahō*

draw near, *appropinquō*

dreadful, *horrendus*

drink, *bibō*

drive, *agitō*

dry, *āridus*

dry up, *torreō*

dust, *pulvis*

dusty, *pulvereus*

dwarf, *nānus*

dwelling, *tectum*

E

eagle, *aquila*

ear, *auris*

earn, *mereō*

earth, *terra*

eat, *edō*

eddy, *gurges*

egg, *ōvum*

eight, *octō*

eighth, *octāvus*

elephant, *elephantus*

emptiness, *vastitās*

enchanted, *venēnātus*

enemy (of one's country), *hostis*

entrust, *mandō*

err, *errō*

error, *error*

even, *vel*

evening, *vesper*

evening star, *vesper*

evidence, *argūmentum*

evil, *malus*

example, *exemplum*

expensive, *sumptuōsus*

experience, *sentiō*

experienced, *perītus*

explore, *explōrō*

explorer, *explōrātor*

expression, *vultus*

eye, *oculus*

F

fable, *fābula*

face, *faciēs, vultus*

fair, *iūstus*

faith, *fidēs*

faithful, *fīdus*

fall (n.), *autumnus*

fall (down), *occidō*

family, *familia*

famine, *famēs*

fang, *dens*

far away, *longinquus*

farmer, *agricola*

farthest, *ultimus*

fast, *citus*

fate, *fātum*

father, *pater*

fault, *culpa*

favor, *benevolentia*

favorite, *cārus*

feast, *epulae*

feather, *pinna*

feeble, *aeger*

feel, *sentiō*

fellow-traveler, *comes*

fence, *saepēs*

few, *paucī*

field, *ager*

fierce, *ferus*

fifth, *quintus*

fight (n.), *proelium*

fight (v.), *pugnō*

figure, *faciēs*

fill (up), *compleō*

find, *inveniō*

finger, *digitus*

fingernail, *unguis*

fire, *ignis*

firebrand, *fax*

firewood, *lignum*

firm, *firmus*

first, *prīmus*

five, *quinque*

fix, *reparō*

flame, *flamma*

flank, *latus*

flee, *fugiō*

fleece, *coma*

fleet (of ships), *classis*

flesh, *carō*

flock, *grex*

flour, *farīna*

flower, *flōs*

fly, *volō*

foe (of one's country), *hostis*

food, *cibus*

foolish, *stultus*

foolishly, *stultē*

footprint, *vestīgium*

forefinger, *index*

foremost, *prīmus*

forest, *silva*

form, *faciēs*

fountain, *fōns*

four, *quattuor*

fourth, *quartus*

fox, *vulpēs*

friend, *amīcus*

frighten, *terreō*

frightened, *trepidus*

frost, *gelū*

frosty, *gelidus*

fungus, *fungus*

funny, *rīdiculus*

G

game, *lūdus*

gangster, *latrō*

garden, *hortus*

garment, *vestis*

gather, *legō*

general, *dux*

generous, *generōsus*

get up, *surgō*

gift, *dōnum*

giraffe, *camēlopardalis*

girl, *puella*

give, *dō*

glad, *laetus*

gladden, *hilarō*

gladiator, *gladiātor*

gloomy place, *tenebrae*

glow, *candeō*

goal, *mēta*

gold, *aurum*

good, *bonus*

good will, *benevolentia*

govern, *regnō, gubernō*

grain, *frūmentum*

grape, *ūva*

grass, *grāmen*

grateful, *grātus*

great, *magnus*

greed, *avāritia*

greenery, *grāmen*

ground, *humus*

grove, *lūcus*

guard, *custōs*

guest, *hospes*

guide, *dux, explōrātor*

gulf, *gurges*

gun, *sclopētum*

H

hair, *capillus, coma*

hand, *manus*

handsome, *pulcher*

happiness, *gaudium*

happy, *laetus*

hard, *dūrus*

hardship, *labor*

harrass, *vexō*

harsh, *acerbus, asper*

hasten, *properō*

hat, *petasus*

hatchet, *secūris*

have, *habeō*

head, *caput*

healthy, *firmus*

hear, *audiō*

heart, *cor*

heaven, *caelum*

heavy, *ponderōsus*

hedge, *saepēs*

hedgehog, *ēricius*

herd, *grex*

herdsman, *armentārius*

hero, *hērōs*

hidden, *obscūrus*

hide, *occultō*

hideout, *latebra*

hiding place, *latebra*

high, *celsus*

high point, *culmen*

highwayman, *latrō*

hill, *collis*

hippo, hippopotamus, *hippopotamus*

hoarse, *raucus*

hold, *habeō, teneō*

hole, *cavum*

hollow, *lacus*

home, *domus*

hoof, *unguis*

hope, *spēs*

horn, *cornū*

horrible, *horrendus*

horse, *equus*

host, *hospes*

hot, *calidus*

hour, *hōra*

house, *domus*

household, *familia*

human being, *homō*

hunger, *famēs*

hungry, *famēlicus*

hunter, *vēnātor*

huntsman, *vēnātor*

hurry, *properō*

husband, *coniunx*

I

ice, *glaciēs*

icy, *gelidus*

ignorant, *ignārus*

image, *effigiēs*

impartial, *iūstus*

in, *in (with abl.)*

inch, *digitus*

influence, *auctōritās*

informer, *index*

inhabitant, *incola*

intelligent, *acūtus*

into, *in (with acc.)*

invite, *vocō*

island, *insula*

J

jail, *carcer*

javelin, *verū*

journey, *iter*

joy, *gaudium*

joyful, *laetus*

judge, *iūdex*

jump, *saliō*

juror, *iūdex*

just, *iūstus*

K

keep, *teneō*

kick, *calcitrō*

kindle, *incendō*

king, *rēx*

kiss, *osculum*

knee, *genū*

know, *sciō*

L

lair, *latebra*

lake, *lacus*

lamp, *lūcerna*

land, *terra*

lard, *lardum*

large, *magnus*

last, *ultimus*

late, *sērus*

laugh, *rīdeō*

laurel tree, *laurus*

law, *lex*

lead, *dūcō*

leader, *dux*

leap, *saliō*

leaves, *coma*

left, *sinister*

leg, *crūs*

legend, *fābula*

legion, *legiō*

letter (correspondence), *litterae;* letter (of the alphabet), *littera*

lettuce, *lactūca*

level area, *campus*

lie hidden, *lateō*

life, *vīta*

lift, *tollō*

light, *lux*

lightning, *fulmen*

likeness, *effigiēs*

limit, *mēta*

lion, *leō*

little, *parvus, paucī*

load, *onus*

lofty, *arduus, celsus*

lone, *sōlus*

long, *longinquus*

long for, *cupiō*

look at, *spectō*

lord, *dominus*

loud, *clārus*

love, *amō*

lurk, *lateō*

M

magical, *magicus*

maid, *famula*

maiden, *virgō*

make, *faciō*

make a noise, *sonō*

make clear, *dēclārō*

man, *homō, vir*

mane, *coma*

manliness, *virtūs*

many, *multus*

marble, *marmor*

mark, *macula*

marketplace, *forum*

master, *dominus*

meal, *cēna*

meat, *carō*

medicine, *medicīna*

meet together, *conveniō*

melon, *mēlo*

mention, *dīcō*

merchant, *mercātor*

mercy, *misericordia*

messenger, *nuntius*

midday, *merīdiēs*

milk, *lac*

millstone, *mola*

mine, *meus*

mirror, *speculum*

mistake, *error*

mob, *caterva*

moist, *ūmidus*

money, *argentum,*
    pecūnia

monkey, *sīmia*

month, *mensis*

moon, *lūna*

mother, *māter*

mountain, *mōns*

mouse, *mūs*

mouth, *ōs*

much, *multus*

mud, *līmus*

mushroom, *fungus*

my, *meus*

N

nape (of neck), *cervix*

narrow pass, *angustiae*

narrows, *angustiae*

nation, *populus*

neck, *cervix, collum*

net, *rēte*

nerve, *nervus*

never, *numquam*

new, *novus*

night, *nox*

nine, *novem*

ninth, *nōnus*

noble, *generōsus*

noon, *merīdiēs*

nose, *nāsus*

not, *nōn*

now, *nunc*

nut, *nucleus*

O

old man, *senex*

on, *in* (with abl.)

on account of, *propter*
    (with acc.)

one, *unus*

only (adj.), *sōlus*

only (adv.), *sōlum*

open, *aperiō*

opinion, *sententia*

or, *vel*

ostrich, *strūthiocamēlus*

ought, *dēbeō*

our(s), *noster*

outlaw, *proscrīptus*

owe, *dēbeō*

ox, *bōs*

P

pace, *gradus*

painful, *acerbus*

pale, *albus*

palm (of the hand),
    palma

palm tree, *palma*

parch, *torreō*

parrot, *psittacus*

part, *pars*

peaceful, *quiētus*

peak, *culmen*

penalty, *poena*

people, *populus*

pepper, *piper*

period of time, *diēs*

person, *homō*

pick, *legō*

pick up, *tollō*

piece, *pars*

pilot, *gubernō*

pirate, *pīrāta*

pity, *misericordia*

place (n.), *locus*

place (v.), *pōnō*

plain, *campus*

plate, *patella*

play (v.), *lūdō;* (an
    instrument), *cantō*

play (n.), *lūdus*

please, *placeō*

pleasing, *grātus*

poem, *carmen*

point (esp. of a spear),
    cuspis

point out, *dēmonstrō*

pointed, *acūtus*

poisoned, *venēnātus*

powder, *pulvis*

power, *auctōritās*

praise (n.), *laus*

praise (v.), *laudō*

prepare, *parō*

preserve, *conservō*

prince, *rēgulus*

prison, *carcer*

prisoner, *captīvus*

prize, *praemium*

proceed, *pergō*

proof, *argūmentum*

proper, *dexter*

province, *prōvincia*

public, *publicus*

public officer, *aedīlis*

public square, *forum*

pull, *trahō*

punishment, *poena*

purchase, *emō*

put, *pōnō*

put something around
    something, *circumdō*

Q

quail, *coturnix*

queen, *rēgīna*

quick, *citus*

quickly, *celeriter*

quiet, *quiētus*

R

rabbit, *cunīculus*

race, *cursus*

raft, *ratis*

rain, *imber*

rainbow, *arcus*

raise, *tollō*

rampart, *vallum*

rat, *mūs*

read, *legō*

read aloud, *recitō*

receive, *accipiō, capiō*

recite, *recitō*

recount, *narrō*

red, *ruber*

region, *regiō*

reign, *regnō*

relate, *narrō*

repair, *reparō*

report, *fāma*

resound, *sonō*

restore, *reparō*

reward, *praemium*

riches, *dīvitiae*

ride (a horse/horseback), *equitō*

right, *dexter, iūstus*

rigid, *sevērus*

ring, *ānulus*

rise, *surgō*

river, *fluvius*

road, *iter, via*

roar, *rudō*

robber, *latrō*

rock, *lapis*

roof, *tectum*

rope, *fūnis*

rough, *asper*

round, *rotundus*

route, *iter*

rug, *lōdix*

rule, *regnō*

rumor, *fāma*

run, *currō*

run away, *fugiō*

S

safe, *salvus*

sail, *nāvigō*

salt, *sāl*

sample, *exemplum*

sand, *harēna*

sandal, *crepida*

save, *conservō*

say, *dīcō*

scale (of an animal), *squāma*

school, *lūdus*

scout, *explōrātor*

sea, *mare*

search out, *explōrō*

seasoning, *condīmentum*

seat, *sella*

second, *secundus*

second time, a (adv.), *iterum*

secret, *arcanum*

secure, *salvus*

see, *videō*

sell, *vendō*

send, *mittō*

serpent, *serpēns*

servant (female), *famula*

servant (male), *famulus*

set on fire, *incendō*

settler, *incola*

seven, *septem*

seventh, *septimus*

severe, *sevērus*

shadows, *tenebrae*

shake, *vexō*

shape, *faciēs*

sharp, *acūtus*

shatter, *frangō*

sheep, *ovis*

shepherd, *pastor*

sheriff, *aedīlis*

shield, *scūtum*

shine, *lūceō*

ship, *nāvis*

shore, *lītus*

shout, *clāmō*

show, *dēmonstrō*

sick, *aeger*

side, *latus*

sight, *vīsus*

sign, *index*

silly, *stultus*

silver, *argentum*

sin (n.), *culpa, dēlictum*

sin (v.), *peccō*

sinew, *nervus*

sing, *cantō*

sister, *soror*

sit, *sedeō*

six, *sex*

sixth, *sextus*

skilled, *perītus*

skip, *saliō*

sky, *caelum*

sleep, *dormiō*

sleeping, *quiētus*

slipper, *crepida*

slow, *tardus*

slow down, *tardō*

slowly, *tardē*

sly, *callidus*

small, *parvus*

smash, *frangō*

smoke, *fūmus*

snake, *serpēns*

snow, *nix*

snow white, *niveus*

snowy, *niveus*

soil, *humus*

soldier, *mīles*

song, *carmen*

soon, *mox*

sound, *sonō*

soup, *iūs*

source, *fōns*

speak, *dīcō*

spend the winter, *hiemō*

spice, *condīmentum*

spit (for roasting meat), *verū*

spot, *macula*

spouse, *coniunx*

spring (season), *vēr*

spring (water source), *fōns*

squirrel, *sciūrus*

stag, *cervus*

stain, *macula*

stand, *stō*

star, *astrum*

starvation, *famēs*

statue, *effigiēs*

steep, *arduus*

steer, *gubernō*

step, *gradus*

stone, *lapis*

storm, *tempestās*

story, *fābula*

strange, *mīrus*

street, *via*

strength, *virtūs*

strict, *sevērus*

strike, *pulsō*

strong, *firmus*

sugar, *sacchārum*

summer, *aestās*

summon, *vocō*

sun, *sōl*

supply, *cōpia*

suspicious, *suspīciōsus*

swamp, *palūs*

swear, *iūrō*

swiftly, *celeriter*

swim, *nō*

sword, *gladius*

T

table, *mensa*

tail, *cauda*

take, *capiō*

take an oath, *iūrō*

take care, *caveō*

taste, *gustō*

teach, *doceō*

tell, *dīcō, narrō*

ten, *decem*

tendon, *nervus*

tenth, *decimus*

terrify, *terreō*

testimony, *testimōnium*

thick, *densus*

thing, *rēs*

third, *tertius*

three, *trēs*

threshold, *līmen*

through, *per (with acc.)*

throw, *iaciō*

thumb, *pollex*

thunderbolt, *fulmen*

tiger, *tīgris*

timber, *lignum*

time, *tempus*

tired, *fessus*

to, *ad (with acc.)*

today, *hodiē*

toenail, *unguis*

toil, *labor*

tomorrow, *crās*

tooth, *dens*

top, *culmen*

torch, *fax*

tortoise, *testūdō*

toss, *vexō*

tough, *dūrus*

toward, *ad (with acc.)*

tower, *turris*

town, *oppidum*

trace, *vestīgium*

track, *vestīgium*

trader, *mercātor*

tree, *arbor*

trek, *iter*

trembling, *trepidus*

trick, *dēcipiō*

troops, *cōpiae*

trust, *fidēs*

trustworthy, *fīdus*

tub, *lacus*

turning point, *mēta*

turret, *turris*

tusk, *dens*

two, *duo*

tyrant, *tyrannus*

U

understand, *sciō*

unicorn, *monocerōs*

unimportant, *parvus*

uninjured, *salvus*

unite, *conciliō*

urge, *urgeō*

V

valley, *vallēs*

vegetable, *holus*

victor, *victor*

view, *vīsus*

vulture, *vultur*

W

wagon, *carrus*

walk, *ambulō*

wall, *vallum*

wander, *errō*

want, *cupiō*

warm, *calidus*

watch (n.), *hōrologium*

watch (v.), *spectō*

watchman, *custōs*

water, *aqua*

way, *via*

wealth, *dīvitiae*

wear, *gerō*

weary, *fessus*

weather, *tempestās*

weight, *onus*

well, *bene*

wet, *ūmidus*

wheel, *rota*

whirlpool, *gurges*

white, *albus*

wicked, *malus*

wife, *coniunx*

wild, *ferus*

wilderness, *vastitās*

win over, *conciliō*

wind, *ventus*

window, *fenestra*

wine, *vīnum*

wing, *āla*

winner, *victor*

winter, *hiems*

wish for, *cupiō*

wit, *sāl*

witch, *venēfica*

with, *cum (with abl.)*

without, *sine (with abl.)*

wolf, *lupus*

woman, *mulier*

wonderful, *mīrus*

wood, *lignum*

work, *labor*

worm, *vermis*

wound (n.), *vulnus*

wound (v.), *vulnerō*

wrong (adj.), *sinister*

wrong (n.), *dēlictum*

Y

year, *annus*

yellow, *flāvus*

yesterday, *herī*

young man,
    adulēscēns, iuvenis

young person,
    adulēscēns, iuvenis

young woman,
    adulēscēns, virgō,
    iuvenis

your(s), *tuus (sg.);*
    vester (pl.)

LATIN-ENGLISH GLOSSARY

A

accipiō, accipere, accēpī, acceptum *I accept, receive* [Wk. 19]

accūsō, accūsāre, accūsāvī, accūsātum *I accuse, blame* [Wk. 25]

acerbus, -a, -um *bitter, harsh, painful* [Wk. 14]

acūtus, -a, -um *sharp, pointed, intelligent* [Wk. 7]

ad (with acc.) *to, toward* [Wk. 26]

adulēscēns, adulēscēntis (m/f) *young man, young woman, young person* [Wk. 14]

aedificium, -ī (n) *building* [Wk. 6]

aedīlis, aedīlis (m) *sheriff, public officer* [Wk. 21]

aeger, aegra, aegrum *sick, feeble* [Wk. 15]

aestās, aestātis (f) *summer* [Wk. 30]

ager, agrī (m) *field* [Wk. 23]

agitō, agitāre, agitāvī, agitātum *I drive, arouse, disturb* [Wk. 5]

agō, agere, ēgī, actum *I do, act* [Wk. 29]

agricola, -ae (m) *farmer* [Wk. 18]

āla, -ae (f) *wing* [Wk. 3]

albus, -a, -um *white, pale* [Wk. 11]

ambulō, ambulāre, ambulāvī, ambulātum *I walk* [Wk. 17]

amīcus, -ī (m) *friend* [Wk. 19]

amō, amāre, amāvī, amātum *I love* [Wk. 1]

angustiae, -ārum (f, pl.) *narrows, narrow pass, difficulties* [Wk. 26]

animal, animālis (n) *animal* [Wk. 10]

annus, -ī (m) *year* [Wk. 30]

ante (with acc.) *before* [Wk. 26]

antrum, -ī (n) *cave* [Wk. 9]

ānulus, -ī (m) *ring* [Wk. 2]

aperiō, aperīre, aperuī, apertum *I open* [Wk. 20]

appropinquō, appropinquāre, appropinquāvī, appropinquātum (with *ad* + acc.) *I approach, draw near* [Wk. 27]

aqua, -ae (f) *water* [Wk. 20]

aquila, -ae (f) *eagle* [Wk. 26]

arbor, arboris (f) *tree* [Wk. 18]

arca, -ae (f) *box, chest* [Wk. 28]

arcanum, -ī (n) *secret* [Wk. 28]

architectus, -ī (m) *architect* [Wk. 18]

arcus, -ūs (m) *bow, arch, rainbow* [Wk. 4]

ardeō, ardēre, arsī, — *I blaze, burn* [Wk. 5]

arduus, -a, -um *steep, lofty* [Wk. 26]

argentum, -ī (n) *silver, money* [Wk. 2]

argūmentum, -ī (n) *proof, evidence* [Wk. 13]

āridus, -a, -um *dry* [Wk. 21]

ariēna, -ae (f) *banana* [Wk. 27]

armentārius, -ī (m) *cowboy, herdsman* [Wk. 21]

asper, aspera, asperum *rough, harsh* [Wk. 15]

astrum, -ī (n) *star, constellation* [Wk. 3]

auctōritās, auctōritātis (f) *authority, influence, power* [Wk. 13]

audācia, -ae (f) *boldness, courage* [Wk. 1]

audiō, audīre, audīvī, audītum *I hear* [Wk. 17]

auris, auris (f) *ear* [Wk. 17]

aurum, -ī (n) *gold* [Wk. 3]

autumnus, -ī (m) *autumn, fall* [Wk. 30]

avāritia, -ae (f) *greed* [Wk. 3]

avis, avis (f) *bird* [Wk. 10]

B

bene, *well* [Wk. 1]

benevolentia, -ae (f) *favor, good will* [Wk. 19]

bibō, bibere, bibī, bibitum *I drink* [Wk. 12]

bonus, -a, -um *good* [Wk. 7]

bōs, bovis (m/f) *ox, bull, cow* [Wk. 4]

brācchium, -ī (n) *arm* [Wk. 14]

brūnus, -a, -um *brown* [Wk. 11]

būtūrum, -ī (n) *butter* [Wk. 29]

C

caelum, -ī (n) *sky, heaven* [Wk. 26]

caeruleus, -a, -um *blue* [Wk. 11]

calcitrō, calcitrāre, calcitrāvī, calcitrātum *I kick* [Wk. 9]

calidus, -a, -um *warm, hot* [Wk. 16]

callidus, -a, -um *clever, sly, cunning* [Wk. 9]

camēlopardalis, camēlopardalis (f) *giraffe* [Wk. 27]

campus, -ī (m) *plain, athletic field, level area* [Wk. 2]

candeō, candēre, canduī, — *I glow, am white* [Wk. 5]

canis, canis (m/f) *dog* [Wk. 10]

cantō, cantāre, cantāvī, cantātum *I sing, play (an instrument)* [Wk. 22]

capillus, -ī (m) *hair* [Wk. 2]

capiō, capere, cēpī, captum *I take, receive, capture, catch* [Wk. 18]

captīvus, -ī (m) *captive, prisoner* [Wk. 28]

caput, capitis (n) *head* [Wk. 27]

carcer, carceris (m) *prison, jail* [Wk. 15]

carmen, carminis (n) *song, chant, poem* [Wk. 22]

carō, carnis (f) *meat, flesh* [Wk. 29]

carrus, -ī (m) *cart, wagon (two-wheeled)* [Wk. 1]

cārus, -a, -um *dear, beloved, favorite* [Wk. 10]

cāseus, -ī (m) *cheese* [Wk. 11]

castellum, -ī (n) *castle* [Wk. 25]

caterva, -ae (f) *crowd, mob* [Wk. 6]

cauda, -ae (f) *tail* [Wk. 27]

caveō, cavēre, cāvī, cautum *I am wary of, take care, am on guard against* [Wk. 10]

cavum, -ī (n) *hole* [Wk. 20]

celeriter, *quickly, swiftly* [Wk. 14]

celsus, -a, -um *lofty, high* [Wk. 9]

cēna, -ae (f) *dinner, meal* [Wk. 11]

cervix, cervīcis (f) *neck, nape (of neck)* [Wk. 2]

cervus, -ī (m) *stag, deer* [Wk. 22]

cibus, -ī (m) *food* [Wk. 11]

cinis, cineris (m) *ashes, destruction* [Wk. 1]

circumdō, circumdāre, circumdedī, circumdatum, *I put something (acc.) around something (dat.)* [Wk. 23]

citus, -a, -um *fast, quick* [Wk. 6]

cīvis, cīvis (m/f) *citizen* [Wk. 15]

clāmō, clāmāre, clāmāvī, clāmātum *I shout* [Wk. 21]

clārus, -a, -um *clear, loud, bright* [Wk. 5]

classis, classis (f) *fleet (of ships)* [Wk. 15]

collis, collis (m) *hill* [Wk. 9]

collum, -ī (n) *neck* [Wk. 1]

coma, -ae (f) *hair, leaves, fleece, mane* [Wk. 5]

comes, comitis (m) *companion, fellow-traveler* [Wk. 18]

compleō, complēre, complēvī, complētum *I fill, fill up* [Wk. 14]

conciliō, conciliāre, conciliāvī, conciliātum *I win over, unite* [Wk. 13]

condīmentum, -ī (n) *spice, seasoning* [Wk. 29]

coniunx, coniugis (m/f) *spouse, wife, husband* [Wk. 7]

conservō, conservāre, conservāvī, conservātum *I save, preserve* [Wk. 13]

conveniō, convenīre, convēnī, conventum *I meet together, come together* [Wk. 18]

convocō, convocāre, convocāvī, convocātum *I call together* [Wk. 7]

cōpia, -ae (f) *supply; pl., troops, supplies* [Wk. 25]

coquō, coquere, coxī, coctum *I cook, bake* [Wk. 29]

coquus, -ī (m) *cook, chef* [Wk. 18]

cor, cordis (n) *heart* [Wk. 22]

cornū, -ūs (n) *horn* [Wk. 4]

corōna, -ae (f) *crown* [Wk. 32]

coturnix, coturnīcis (f) *quail* [Wk. 5]

crās, *tomorrow* [Wk. 12]

creō, creāre, creāvī, creātum *I create* [Wk. 30]

crepida, -ae (f) *slipper, sandal* [Wk. 28]

crocodīlus, -ī (m) *crocodile* [Wk. 27]

crūs, crūris (n) *leg* [Wk. 14]

culmen, culminis (n) *top, peak, high point* [Wk. 26]

culpa, -ae (f) *fault, blame, sin* [Wk. 1]

cum (with abl.) *with* [Wk. 28]

cunīculus, -ī (m) *rabbit* [Wk. 12]

cupiō, cupere, cupīvī, cupītum *I want, long for, wish for* [Wk. 19]

cūriōsus, -a, -um *curious, diligent* [Wk. 8]

currō, currere, cucurrī, cursum *I run* [Wk. 1]

cursus, -ūs (m) *race* [Wk. 17]

cuspis, cuspidis (f) *point (esp. of a spear)* [Wk. 2]

custōs, custōdis (m/f) *guard, watchman* [Wk. 7]

D

damnō, damnāre, damnāvī, damnātum *I condemn* [Wk. 13]

dēbeō, dēbēre, dēbuī, dēbitum *I owe, ought* [Wk. 2]

decem, *ten* [Wk. 30]

decimus, -a, -um *tenth* [Wk. 31]

dēcipiō, dēcipere, dēcēpī, dēceptum *I trick, deceive* [Wk. 28]

dēclārō, dēclārāre, dēclārāvī, dēclārātum *I declare, make clear* [Wk. 23]

dēlectō, dēlectāre, dēlectāvī, dēlectātum *I delight* [Wk. 5]

dēlictum, -ī (n) *crime, sin, wrong* [Wk. 13]

dēmonstrō, dēmonstrāre, dēmonstrāvī, dēmonstrātum *I show, point out* [Wk. 6]

dens, dentis (m) *tooth, tusk, fang* [Wk. 9]

densus, -a, -um *dense, thick* [Wk. 3]

dexter, dextra, dextrum *right (as opposed to left), proper* [Wk. 32]

dīcō, dīcere, dīxī, dīctum *I say, speak, tell, mention* [Wk. 15]

diēs, diēī (m) *day, period of time* [Wk. 12]

digitus, -ī (m) *finger, inch* [Wk. 2]

dīvitiae, -ārum (f, pl.) *riches, wealth* [Wk. 28]

dō, dare, dedī, datum *I give* [Wk. 11]

doceō, docēre, docuī, doctum *I teach* [Wk. 20]

dominus, -ī (m) *master, lord* [Wk. 6]

domus, -ūs (f) *home, house* [Wk. 31]

dōnum, -ī (n) *gift* [Wk. 11]

dormiō, dormīre, dormīvī, dormītum *I sleep* [Wk. 17]

dracō, dracōnis (m) *dragon* [Wk. 9]

dūcō, dūcere, dūxī, ductum *I lead* [Wk. 1]

duo, -ae, -o *two* [Wk. 30]

dūrus, -a, -um *hard, tough, difficult* [Wk. 27]

dux, ducis (m) *leader, guide, general* [Wk. 15]

E

edō, edere, ēdī, ēsum *I eat* [Wk. 12]

effigiēs, effigiēī (f) *image, likeness, statue* [Wk. 12]

elephantus, -ī (m/f) *elephant* [Wk. 24]

emō, emere, ēmī, emptum *I buy, purchase* [Wk. 6]

epulae, -ārum (f, pl.) *feast* [Wk. 6]

equitō, equitāre, equitāvī, equitātum *I ride (a horse), ride horseback* [Wk. 21]

equus, -ī (m) *horse* [Wk. 5]

ēricius, -ī (m) *hedgehog* [Wk. 20]

errō, errāre, errāvī, errātum *I wander, err, am mistaken* [Wk. 10]

error, errōris (m) *error, mistake* [Wk. 32]

et, *and* [Wk. 4]

exemplum, -ī (n) *example, sample* [Wk. 23]

exercitus, -ūs (m) *army* [Wk. 4]

explōrātor, explōrātōris (m) *explorer, scout, guide* [Wk. 18]

explōrō, explōrāre, explōrāvī, explōrātum *I search out, explore* [Wk. 7]

F

fābula, -ae (f) *story, legend, fable* [Wk. 15]

faciēs, faciēī (f) *shape, form, figure, face* [Wk. 13]

faciō, facere, fēcī, factum *I make, do, build* [Wk. 18]

fāma, -ae (f) *report, rumor* [Wk. 19]

famēlicus, -a, -um *hungry* [Wk. 21]

famēs, famis (f) *famine, hunger, starvation* [Wk. 25]

familia, -ae (f) *household, family* [Wk. 28]

famula, -ae (f) *maid, servant (female)* [Wk. 6]

famulus, -ī (m) *servant (male)* [Wk. 6]

farīna, -ae (f) *flour* [Wk. 29]

fātum, -ī (n) *fate, destiny* [Wk. 21]

fax, facis (f) *torch, firebrand* [Wk. 23]

fēlēs, fēlis (f) *cat* [Wk. 10]

fenestra, -ae (f) *window* [Wk. 1]

ferus, -a, -um *fierce, wild* [Wk. 4]

fessus, -a, -um *tired, weary* [Wk. 6]

fidēs, fideī (f) *faith, trust* [Wk. 12]

fīdus, -a, -um *faithful, trustworthy* [Wk. 7]

firmus, -a, -um *firm, strong, healthy* [Wk. 14]

flamma, -ae (f) *flame* [Wk. 7]

flāvus, -a, -um *yellow, blond* [Wk. 11]

flōs, flōris (m) *flower* [Wk. 5]

fluvius, -ī (m) *river* [Wk. 2]

fodiō, fodere, fōdī, fossum *I dig* [Wk. 20]

fōns, fontis (m) *spring, fountain, source* [Wk. 10]

forum, -ī (n) *public square, marketplace* [Wk. 28]

frangō, frangere, frēgī, fractum *I break, smash, shatter* [Wk. 14]

frāter, frātris (m) *brother* [Wk. 31]

frūmentum, -ī (n) *grain, (pl.) crops* [Wk. 6]

fugiō, fugere, fūgī, fugitum *I run away, flee* [Wk. 18]

fulmen, fulminis (n) *thunderbolt, lightning* [Wk. 5]

fūmus, -ī (m) *smoke* [Wk. 3]

fungus, -ī (m) *mushroom, fungus* [Wk. 20]

fūnis, fūnis (m) *rope* [Wk. 23]

G

gaudium, gaudiī (n) *joy, happiness* [Wk. 22]

gelidus, -a, -um *cold, icy, frosty* [Wk. 8]

gelū, -ūs (n) *chill, frost* [Wk. 4]

generōsus, -a, -um *generous, noble* [Wk. 28]

genū, -ūs (n) *knee* [Wk. 4]

gerō, gerere, gessī, gestum *I wear, bear* [Wk. 21]

glaciēs, glaciēī (f) *ice* [Wk. 13]

gladiātor, gladiātōris (m) *gladiator* [Wk. 4]

gladius, -ī (m) *sword* [Wk. 26]

gradus, -ūs (m) *step, pace* [Wk. 4]

grāmen, grāminis (n) *grass, greenery* [Wk. 18]

grātus, -a, -um *grateful, pleasing, agreeable* [Wk. 14]

grex, gregis (m) *flock, herd* [Wk. 8]

gubernō, gubernāre, gubernāvī, gubernātum *I pilot, steer, govern* [Wk. 15]

gurges, gurgitis (m) *whirlpool, eddy, gulf* [Wk. 16]

gustō, gustāre, gustāvī, gustātum *I taste* [Wk. 11]

H

habeō, habēre, habuī, habitum *I have, hold* [Wk. 6]

harēna, -ae (f) *sand* [Wk. 5]

herī, *yesterday* [Wk. 12]

hērōs, hērōis (m) *hero* [Wk. 2]

hiemō, hiemāre, hiemāvī, hiemātum *I spend the winter* [Wk. 28]

hiems, hiemis (f) *winter* [Wk. 30]

hilarō, hilarāre, hilarāvī, hilarātum *I cheer up, gladden* [Wk. 28]

hippopotamus, -ī (m) *hippopotamus, hippo* [Wk. 27]

hodiē, *today* [Wk. 12]

holus, holeris (n) *vegetable* [Wk. 18]

homō, hominis (m) *person, man, human being* [Wk. 23]

hōra, -ae (f) *hour* [Wk. 31]

hōrologium, hōrologiī (n) *clock, watch* [Wk. 12]

horrendus, -a, -um *horrible, dreadful, awful* [Wk. 3]

hortus, -ī (m) *garden* [Wk. 6]

hospes, hospitis (m) *guest, host* [Wk. 19]

hostis, hostis (m/f) *enemy, foe (of one's country)* [Wk. 9]

humus, -ī (f) *ground, soil* [Wk. 3]

I

iaciō, iacere, iēcī, iactum *I throw* [Wk. 20]

ignārus, -a, -um *ignorant* [Wk. 13]

ignis, ignis (m) *fire* [Wk. 16]

imber, imbris (m) *rain* [Wk. 20]

in (with acc.) *into* [Wk. 25]

in (with abl.) *in, on* [Wk. 28]

incendō, incendere, incendī, incensum *I kindle, set on fire* [Wk. 16]

incola, -ae (m/f) *inhabitant, settler, colonist* [Wk. 3]

index, indicis (m) *informer, sign, forefinger* [Wk. 2]

insula, -ae (f) *island* [Wk. 16]

inveniō, invenīre, invēnī, inventum *I find, discover, come upon* [Wk. 17]

īrātus, -a, -um *angry* [Wk. 14]

iter, itineris (n) *journey, road, route, trek* [Wk. 10]

iterum, *again, a second time* [Wk. 22]

iūdex, iūdicis (m) *judge, juror* [Wk. 13]

iūrō, iūrāre, iūrāvī, iūrātum *I swear, take an oath* [Wk. 13]

iūs, iūris (n) *soup* [Wk. 18]

iūstus, -a, -um *just, right, fair, impartial* [Wk. 13]

iuvenis, iuvenis (m/f) *young person, young man, young woman* [Wk. 23]

L

labor, labōris (m) *work, toil, hardship* [Wk. 19]

lac, lactis (n) *milk* [Wk. 11]

lactūca, -ae (f) *lettuce* [Wk. 11]

lacus, lacūs (m) *lake, tub, hollow* [Wk. 25]

laetus, -a, -um *happy, joyful, glad* [Wk. 7]

lapis, lapidis (m) *stone, rock* [Wk. 5]

lardum, -ī (n) *bacon, lard* [Wk. 11]

latebra, -ae (f) *hiding place, hideout, lair* [Wk. 26]

lateō, latēre, latuī, — *I lie hidden, lurk, am concealed* [Wk. 15]

latrō, latrōnis (m) *gangster, robber, highwayman* [Wk. 13]

latus, lateris (n) *flank, side* [Wk. 4]

laudō, laudāre, laudāvī, laudātum *I praise* [Wk. 11]

laurus, -ī (f) *laurel tree* [Wk. 3]

laus, laudis (f) *praise* [Wk. 17]

lectus, -ī (m) *couch, bed* [Wk. 7]

legiō, legiōnis (f) *legion* [Wk. 25]

legō, legere, lēgī, lectum *I gather, pick, read* [Wk. 16]

leō, leōnis (m) *lion* [Wk. 4]

lex, lēgis (f) *law* [Wk. 21]

līberī, līberōrum (m, pl.) *children* [Wk. 19]

lignum, -ī (n) *wood, timber, firewood* [Wk. 16]

līmen, līminis (n) *doorway, threshold* [Wk. 25]

līmus, -ī (m) *mud* [Wk. 20]

littera, -ae (f) *letter (of the alphabet); pl., letter (correspondence), letters (of the alphabet)* [Wk. 19]

lītus, lītoris (n) *shore, beach* [Wk. 15]

locus, -ī (m) *place* [Wk. 6]

lōdix, lōdīcis (f) *blanket, rug* [Wk. 28]

longinquus, -a, -um *far away, distant* [Wk. 10]

longus, -a, -um *long* [Wk. 4]

lūceō, lūcēre, lūxī, — *I shine, am bright* [Wk. 2]

lūcerna, -ae (f) *lamp* [Wk. 7]

lūcus, -ī (m) *grove* [Wk. 5]

lūdō, lūdere, lūsī, lūsum *I play* [Wk. 20]

lūdus, -ī (m) *game, play, school* [Wk. 20]

lūna, -ae (f) *moon* [Wk. 31]

lupus, -ī (m) *wolf* [Wk. 21]

lux, lūcis (f) *light* [Wk. 30]

M

macula, -ae (f) *spot, mark, stain* [Wk. 11]

magicus, -a, -um *magical* [Wk. 9]

magnus, -a, -um *large, big, great* [Wk. 10]

mālum, -ī (n) *apple* [Wk. 22]

malus, -a, -um *bad, evil, wicked* [Wk. 7]

mandō, mandāre, mandāvī, mandātum *I entrust, command* [Wk. 23]

manus, -ūs (f) *hand* [Wk. 27]

mare, maris (n) *sea* [Wk. 10]

marmor, marmoris (n) *marble* [Wk. 23]

māter, mātris (f) *mother* [Wk. 19]

medicīna, -ae (f) *medicine* [Wk. 14]

medicus, -ī (m) *doctor, dentist* [Wk. 14]

mēlēs, mēlis (f) *badger* [Wk. 20]

mēlo, mēlōnis (m) *melon* [Wk. 27]

mensa, -ae (f) *table* [Wk. 7]

mensis, mensis (m) *month* [Wk. 31]

mercātor, mercātōris (m) *merchant, trader* [Wk. 7]

mereō, merēre, meruī, meritum *I deserve, earn, am worthy of* [Wk. 3]

merīdiēs, merīdiēī (m) *noon, midday* [Wk. 12]

mēta, -ae (f) *goal, turning point, limit* [Wk. 17]

meus, -a, -um *my, mine* [Wk. 29]

mīles, mīlitis (m/f) *soldier* [Wk. 25]

mīrus, -a, -um *strange, wonderful* [Wk. 8]

misericordia, -ae (f) *pity, mercy* [Wk. 15]

mittō, mittere, mīsī, missum *I send* [Wk. 21]

mola, -ae (f) *millstone* [Wk. 2]

monocerōs, monocerōtis (m) *unicorn* [Wk. 9]

mōns, mōntis (m) *mountain* [Wk. 10]

mordeō, mordēre, momordī, morsum *I bite* [Wk. 9]

mox, *soon* [Wk. 12]

mulier, mulieris (f) *woman* [Wk. 14]

multus, -a, -um *much, many* [Wk. 19]

mūs, mūris (m/f) *mouse, rat* [Wk. 24]

mūtō, mūtāre, mūtāvī, mūtātum *I change* [Wk. 9]

N

nānus, -ī (m) *dwarf* [Wk. 22]

narrō, narrāre, narrāvī, narrātum *I tell, relate, recount* [Wk. 19]

nāsus, -ī (m) *nose* [Wk. 27]

nāvigō, nāvigāre, nāvigāvī, nāvigātum *I sail* [Wk. 10]

nāvis, nāvis (f) *ship* [Wk. 15]

nervus, -ī (m) *tendon, nerve, sinew* [Wk. 1]

niger, nigra, nigrum *black, dark* [Wk. 11]

niveus, -a, um *snowy, snow white* [Wk. 22]

nix, nivis (f) *snow* [Wk. 22]

nō, nāre, nāvī, — *I swim* [Wk. 15]

nōn, *not* [Wk. 1]

nōnus, -a, -um *ninth* [Wk. 31]

noster, nostra, nostrum *our, ours* [Wk. 29]

novem, *nine* [Wk. 30]

novus, -a, -um *new* [Wk. 7]

nox, noctis (f) *night* [Wk. 9]

nucleus, -ī (m) *nut* [Wk. 20]

numquam, *never* [Wk. 17]

nunc, *now* [Wk. 12]

nuntiō, nuntiāre, nuntiāvī, nuntiātum *I announce* [Wk. 26]

nuntius, -ī (m) *messenger* [Wk. 26]

O

obscūrus, -a, -um *hidden, dark* [Wk. 9]

occidō, occidere, occidī, occāsum *I fall, fall down, die* [Wk. 21]

occultō, occultāre, occultāvī, occultātum *I hide* [Wk. 20]

octāvus, -a, -um *eighth* [Wk. 31]

octō, *eight* [Wk. 30]

oculus, -ī (m) *eye* [Wk. 27]

onus, oneris (n) *burden, load, weight* [Wk. 23]

oppidum, -ī (n) *town* [Wk. 3]

oppugnō, oppugnāre, oppugnāvī, oppugnātum *I attack* [Wk. 9]

ōs, ōris (n) *mouth* [Wk. 1]

osculum, -ī (n) *kiss* [Wk. 22]

ovis, ovis (f) *sheep* [Wk. 18]

ōvum, -ī (n) *egg* [Wk. 29]

P

paene, *almost* [Wk. 10]

palma, -ae (f) *palm (of the hand), palm tree* [Wk. 2]

palūs, palūdis (f) *swamp, bog* [Wk. 26]

pānis, pānis (m) *bread* [Wk. 11]

parō, parāre, parāvī, parātum *I prepare* [Wk. 6]

pars, partis (f) *part, piece* [Wk. 16]

parvus, -a, -um *little, small, unimportant* [Wk. 10]

pastor, pastōris (m) *shepherd* [Wk. 18]

patella, -ae (f) *plate, dish* [Wk. 2]

pater, patris (m) *father* [Wk. 19]

paucī, -ae, -a *few, little* [Wk. 31]

peccō, peccāre, peccāvī, peccātum *I sin* [Wk. 13]

pecūnia, -ae (f) *money* [Wk. 3]

per (with acc.) *through* [Wk. 25]

pergō, pergere, perrexī, perrectum. *I continue, proceed* [Wk. 7]

perīculum, -ī (n) *danger* [Wk. 15]

perītus, -a, -um *skilled, experienced* [Wk. 6]

perniciēs, perniciēī (f) *disaster, destruction* [Wk. 13]

petasus, -ī (m) *hat* [Wk. 21]

pinna, -ae (f) *feather* [Wk. 5]

piper, piperis (n) *pepper* [Wk. 29]

pīrāta, -ae (m) *pirate* [Wk. 15]

placenta, -ae (f) *cake* [Wk. 28]

placeō, placēre, placuī, placitum (with dat.) *I please, am acceptable to* [Wk. 24]

poena, -ae (f) *penalty, punishment* [Wk. 2]

pollex, pollicis (m) *thumb* [Wk. 2]

ponderōsus, -a, -um *heavy* [Wk. 23]

pōnō, pōnere, posuī, positum *I put, place* [Wk. 27]

pōns, pōntis (m) *bridge* [Wk. 18]

populus, -ī (m) *people, nation* [Wk. 14]

portō, portāre, portāvī, portātum *I carry* [Wk. 2]

possum, posse, potuī, — *I am able, can* [Wk. 2]

post (with acc.) *after, behind* [Wk. 26]

postulō, postulāre, postulāvī, postulātum *I demand* [Wk. 23]

praemium, -ī (n) *prize, reward* [Wk. 3]

prīmus, -a, -um *first, foremost* [Wk. 15]

proelium, -ī (n) *battle, fight* [Wk. 15]

properō, properāre, properāvī, properātum *I hurry, hasten, accelerate* [Wk. 1]

propter (with acc.) *on account of, because of* [Wk. 27]

proscrīptus, -ī (m) *outlaw* [Wk. 21]

prōvincia, -ae (f) *province* [Wk. 3]

psittacus, -ī (m) *parrot* [Wk. 15]

publicus, -a, -um *public* [Wk. 7]

puella, -ae (f) *girl* [Wk. 12]

puer, puerī (m) *boy* [Wk. 31]

pugnō, pugnāre, pugnāvī, pugnātum *I fight* [Wk. 4]

pulcher, pulchra, pulchrum *beautiful, handsome* [Wk. 19]

pulsō, pulsāre, pulsāvī, pulsātum *I strike, beat* [Wk. 27]

pulvereus, -a, -um *dusty* [Wk. 21]

pulvis, pulveris (m) *dust, powder* [Wk. 28]

purgō, purgāre, purgāvī, purgātum *I clean, cleanse, clear* [Wk. 14]

Q

quartus, -a, -um *fourth* [Wk. 31]

quattuor, *four* [Wk. 30]

-que, *and* [Wk. 19]

quiētus, -a, -um *quiet, sleeping, peaceful* [Wk. 5]

quinque, *five* [Wk. 30]

quintus, -a, -um *fifth* [Wk. 31]

R

ratis, ratis (f) *raft* [Wk. 10]

raucus, -a, -um *hoarse* [Wk. 6]

recitō, recitāre, recitāvī, recitātum *I read aloud, recite* [Wk. 19]

rēgīna, -ae (f) *queen* [Wk. 12]

regiō, regiōnis (f) *region, direction, area* [Wk. 4]

regnō, regnāre, regnāvī, regnātum *I rule, govern, reign* [Wk. 3]

rēgulus, -ī (m) *prince* [Wk. 22]

reparō, reparāre, reparāvī, reparātum *I fix, repair, restore* [Wk. 14]

rēs, reī (f) *thing* [Wk. 12]

rēte, rētis (n) *net* [Wk. 10]

reus, -ī (m) *defendant* [Wk. 13]

rēx, rēgis (m) *king* [Wk. 12]

rīdeō, rīdēre, rīsī, rīsum *I laugh* [Wk. 2]

rīdiculus, -a, -um *funny, amusing* [Wk. 20]

rogō, rogāre, rogāvī, rogātum *I ask* [Wk. 11]

rota, -ae (f) *wheel* [Wk. 1]

rotundus, -a, -um *round, circular* [Wk. 27]

ruber, rubra, rubrum *red* [Wk. 11]

rudō, rudere, rudīvī, rudītum *I roar, bellow, bray* [Wk. 4]

S

sacchārum, -ī (n) *sugar* [Wk. 29]

saepēs, saepis (f) *hedge, fence* [Wk. 23]

sagitta, -ae (f) *arrow* [Wk. 26]

sāl, salis (m) *salt, wit* [Wk. 29]

saliō, salīre, saluī, saltum *I jump, leap, skip* [Wk. 17]

salvus, -a, -um *safe, secure, uninjured* [Wk. 15]

sanguis, sanguinis (m) *blood* [Wk. 4]

scandō, scandere, scandī, scansum *I climb* [Wk. 18]

sciō, scīre, scīvī, scītum *I know, understand* [Wk. 19]

sciūrus, -ī (m) *squirrel* [Wk. 20]

sclopētum, -ī (n) *gun* [Wk. 21]

scopulus, -ī (m) *cliff, crag* [Wk. 18]

scūtum, -ī (n) *shield* [Wk. 26]

secō, secāre, secuī, sectum *I cut* [Wk. 25]

secundus, -a, -um *second* [Wk. 31]

secūris, secūris (f) *axe, hatchet* [Wk. 23]

sed, *but* [Wk. 9]

sedeō, sedēre, sēdī, sessum *I sit* [Wk. 1]

sella, -ae (f) *seat, chair* [Wk. 7]

semper, *always* [Wk. 23]

senex, senis (m) *old man* [Wk. 23]

sententia, -ae (f) *opinion, decision* [Wk. 13]

sentiō, sentīre, sensī, sensum *I feel, experience* [Wk. 19]

septem, *seven* [Wk. 30]

septimus, -a, -um *seventh* [Wk. 31]

serpēns, serpentis (m/f) *snake, serpent* [Wk. 9]

sērus, -a, -um *late* [Wk. 12]

sevērus, -a, -um *severe, strict, rigid* [Wk. 13]

sex, *six* [Wk. 30]

sextus, -a, -um *sixth* [Wk. 31]

silva, -ae (f) *forest* [Wk. 5]

sīmia, -ae (f) *ape, monkey* [Wk. 27]

simul, *at the same time* [Wk. 17]

sine (with abl.) *without* [Wk. 29]

sinister, sinistra, sinistrum *left, wrong* [Wk. 32]

socius, -ī (m) *companion, associate, ally* [Wk. 14]

sōl, sōlis (m) *sun* [Wk. 31]

sōlum, *only* [Wk. 10]

sōlus, -a, -um *only, alone, lone* [Wk. 21]

sonō, sonāre, sonuī, sonitum *I resound, sound, make a noise* [Wk. 5]

soror, sorōris (f) *sister* [Wk. 31]

spectō, spectāre, spectāvī, spectātum *I watch, look at* [Wk. 9]

speculum, -ī (n) *mirror* [Wk. 22]

spēs, speī (f) *hope* [Wk. 12]

squāma, -ae (f) *scale (of an animal)* [Wk. 9]

stō, stāre, stetī, statum *I stand* [Wk. 25]

strūthiocamēlus, -ī (m) *ostrich* [Wk. 27]

stultē, *foolishly* [Wk. 31]

stultus, -a, -um *foolish, silly* [Wk. 24]

sum, esse, fuī, futūrum *I am* [Wk. 5]

sumptuōsus, -a, -um *expensive* [Wk. 7]

surgō, surgere, surrēxī, surrēctum *I get up, rise* [Wk. 17]

suspīciōsus, -a, -um *suspicious* [Wk. 28]

T

tardē, *slowly* [Wk. 17]

tardō, tardāre, tardāvī, tardātum *I delay, slow down* [Wk. 8]

tardus, -a, -um *slow* [Wk. 17]

tectum, -ī (n) *roof, building, dwelling* [Wk. 25]

terra, -ae (f) *earth, land* [Wk. 30]

tempestās, tempestātis (f) *weather, storm* [Wk. 5]

tempus, temporis (n) *time* [Wk. 12]

tenebrae, tenebrārum (f, pl.) *darkness, gloomy place, shadows* [Wk. 26]

teneō, tenēre, tenuī, tentum *I hold, keep* [Wk. 28]

terreō, terrēre, terruī, territum *I frighten, terrify* [Wk. 5]

tertius, -a, -um *third* [Wk. 31]

testimōnium, -ī (n) *testimony* [Wk. 13]

testūdō, testūdinis (f) *tortoise* [Wk. 17]

tīgris, tīgridis (m/f) *tiger* [Wk. 4]

tollō, tollere, sustulī, sublātum *I pick up, lift, raise* [Wk. 27]

torreō, torrēre, torruī, tostum *I burn, parch, dry up* [Wk. 6]

trahō, trahere, traxī, tractum *I pull, draw, drag* [Wk. 27]

trans (with acc.) *across* [Wk. 25]

trepidus, -a, -um *trembling, anxious, frightened* [Wk. 3]

trēs, tria *three* [Wk. 30]

turris, turris (f) *tower, turret* [Wk. 25]

tussiō, tussīre, tussī, tussītum *I cough* [Wk. 18]

tuus, -a, -um *your, yours (sing.)* [Wk. 29]

tyrannus, -ī (m) *tyrant* [Wk. 23]

U

ultimus, -a, -um *last, farthest* [Wk. 31]

ūmidus, -a, -um *wet, damp, moist* [Wk. 3]

unguis, unguis (m) *fingernail, toenail, claw, hoof* [Wk. 9]

unus, -a, -um *one* [Wk. 30]

urbs, urbis (f) *city* [Wk. 25]

urgeō, urgēre, ursī, ursum *I urge* [Wk. 22]

ūva, -ae (f) *grape* [Wk. 29]

V

vallēs, vallis (f) *valley* [Wk. 25]

vallum, -ī (n) *rampart, wall* [Wk. 26]

vastitās, vastitātis (f) *desert, emptiness, wilderness* [Wk. 21]

vehō, vehere, vexī, vectum *I carry, convey* [Wk. 10]

vel, *or (conj.), even (adv.)* [Wk. 18]

vēnātor, vēnātōris (m) *hunter, huntsman* [Wk. 22]

vendō, vendere, vendidī, venditum *I sell, advertise* [Wk. 7]

venēfica, -ae (f) *witch* [Wk. 22]

venēnātus, -a, -um *poisoned, enchanted* [Wk. 22]

veniō, venīre, vēnī, ventum *I come* [Wk. 26]

ventus, -ī (m) *wind* [Wk. 3]

vēr, vēris (n) *spring* [Wk. 30]

vermis, vermis (m) *worm* [Wk. 20]

verū, -ūs (n) *javelin, spit (for roasting meat)* [Wk. 4]

vesper, vesperis (m) *evening, evening star* [Wk. 30]

vespertīliō, vespertīliōnis (m) *bat* [Wk. 30]

vester, vestra, vestrum *your, yours (pl.)* [Wk. 29]

vestigium, vestīgiī (n) *footprint, trace, track* [Wk. 17]

vestis, vestis (f) *clothing, garment* [Wk. 21]

vexō, vexāre, vexāvī, vexātum *I shake, toss, harrass, annoy* [Wk. 24]

via, -ae (f) *road, street, way* [Wk. 6]

victor, victōris (m) *victor, winner* [Wk. 17]

videō, vidēre, vīdī, vīsum *I see* [Wk. 1]

vincō, vincere, vīcī, victum *I defeat, beat, conquer* [Wk. 17]

vīnum, -ī (n) *wine* [Wk. 11]

vir, virī (m) *man* [Wk. 14]

virgō, virginis (f) *young woman, maiden* [Wk. 14]

virtūs, virtūtis (f) *manliness, courage, strength* [Wk. 25]

vīsus, -ūs (m) *view, sight* [Wk. 8]

vīta, -ae (f) *life* [Wk. 3]

vītō, vītāre, vītāvī, vītātum *I avoid* [Wk. 6]

vocō, vocāre, vocāvī, vocātum *I call, summon, invite* [Wk. 22]

volō, volāre, volāvī, volātum *I fly* [Wk. 26]

vulnerō, vulnerāre, vulnerāvī, vulnerātum *I wound* [Wk. 14]

vulnus, vulneris (n) *wound* [Wk. 4]

vulpēs, vulpis (f) *fox* [Wk. 17]

vultur, vulturis (m) *vulture* [Wk. 21]

vultus, -ūs (m) *face, expression* [Wk. 1]

SOURCES AND HELPS

Brunel Jr., Donald J. *Basic Latin Vocabulary*. Oxford: American Classical League, 1989. In the later stages of developing the curriculum, this was my basic source for choosing and defining vocabulary.

Buehner, William J. and John W. Ambrose. *Introduction to Preparatory Latin,* Book I, 2nd ed. Wellesley Hills: Independent School Press, 1977.

Crane, Gregory R. "Perseus Latin Word Study Tool." http://www. http://www.perseus.tufts.edu/hopper/morph. This site is a searchable, online version of Lewis & Short's *Latin Dictionary* (listed below) and has been invaluable. (Note that when you first visit the site, you will need to change the drop-down box for language to "Latin.")

Ehrlich, Eugene. *Amo, Amas, Amat, and More.* New York: Harper and Row, 1985.

Greenough, J. B., J. H. Allen, et al., *Allen & Greenough's New Latin Grammar.* Boston: Ginn and Co., 1903.

Harper, Douglas. *Online Etymology Dictionary.* http://etymonline.com. The site is a wonderful resource for discovering word roots and a stellar compilation of many etymological sources including the *Oxford English Dictionary, A Comprehensive Etymological Dictionary of the English Language,* and *An Etymological Dictionary of Modern English.*

Lewis, Charlton T. and Charles Short. *A Latin Dictionary.* Oxford: Clarendon Press, 1984 [1879].

Mahoney, Kevin D. "LATdict." http://www.latin-dictionary.net. A great resource for quick, online Latin reference. Does not include macrons.

Mirza, Sumair and Jason Tsang. "Latin Wordstock—Latin Vocabulary and Derivatives." http://www. classicsunveiled.com/romevd/html/index.html. This is a helpful list of derivative possibilities, best paired with an English dictionary for confirmation.

Morris, William, ed. *American Heritage Dictionary of the English Language,* New College Edition. Boston: Houghton Mifflin, 1976. This was my basic reference English dictionary and one I would recommend for the teaching of Latin. My main use for it was to confirm and define derivatives.

Moutoux, Eugene R. "Latin Derivatives: English Words from Latin." http://german-latin-english.com/ latinderivatives.htm. This is another list of derivative possibilities, best paired with an English dictionary for confirmation.

Schaeffer, Rudolph F. *Latin English Derivative Dictionary,* edited by W. C. Carr. Oxford: American Classical League, 1960.

Simpson, D. P. *Cassell's Latin and English Dictionary.* New York: Macmillan Publishing, 1987. This is my most commonly used Latin dictionary, as well as the one the students used in their work.

Weber, Robertus, ed. *Biblia Sacra Vulgata.* Stuttgart: Wurttembergische Bibelanstalt, 1975. I used this and perhaps other versions for Scripture quotations.

Wheelock, Frederic M. *Latin: An Introductory Course Based on Ancient Authors,* 6th ed. revised. New York: Harper and Row, 2005. I depended upon this for Latin grammar, and I would recommend it for Latin teachers who need more of a Latin background.